D0456952

Advance Praise for
SID-IZENS UNITED

"Sid Rosenberg writes the way he talks: fast and blunt. His book is entertaining and provides the reader insight into a guy who hit the bottom but pulled himself up to great success. You'll get your money's worth and more."

—Bill O'Reilly, Media Guy

"Sid Rosenberg is New York personified—caustic, unfiltered, hilarious, and with a huge heart. The bad boy of radio dispenses ripping tales about fame, sports, and politics in his new book. But the sweet bonus is the wisdom he learned from the school of hard knocks on how to succeed at marriage and fatherhood."

—Miranda Devine

"Every person is born with a filter between their brain and their mouth. Sid Rosenberg was born without one. Anything he thinks of he says. Love him or hate him…he's the real deal."

—Chazz Palminteri

"Sid Rosenberg is truly one of a kind—loud, boisterous, opinionated, loyal, heart of gold. Sid's latest book spells it all out: the great successes, the setbacks, and the hard-fought comebacks. A New Yorker to his very essence. I am proud to call Sid my friend. As we Irish say: Sid Rosenberg is a mensch!"

—PETER KING

"I've known Sid since he was a customer service agent for a company nobody ever heard of. The fact that I would care what he has to say about world politics or society as a whole is as shocking to me as it is to you, but here I am laughing and crying while hearing his unmistakably unique voice in my ears as I turn the pages of this book. Sid's a talented creator, an unapologetic and gifted performer in a sea of copycats and unoriginal thoughts. He simply stands out. We share some of the same demons and I'm beyond proud to see him overcome them and succeed as he has and become the father and man that his dad would be so proud of. I have no idea what a Sid-izen is, and I'm terrified now that I might be one."

—CRAIG CARTON

Rosenberg, Sid, 1967-
Sid-Izens United : Salacious
Spiels, Stories, Suggestions,
2022
33305254208279
ca   10/19/22

SALACIOUS SPIELS, STORIES,
SUGGESTIONS, AND SOLUTIONS
TO WITHSTAND A WOKE WORLD

★ ★ SID ★ ★
ROSENBERG

WITH JOHNNY RUSSO

Post Hill
PRESS

A POST HILL PRESS BOOK
ISBN: 978-1-63758-287-9
ISBN (eBook): 978-1-63758-288-6

Sid-izens United:
Salacious Spiels, Stories, Suggestions, and Solutions to Withstand
a Woke World
© 2022 by Sid Rosenberg
All Rights Reserved

Cover design by Cody Corcoran

No part of this book may be reproduced, stored in a retrieval system, or transmitted by any means without the written permission of the author and publisher.

Post Hill Press
New York • Nashville
posthillpress.com

Published in the United States of America
1 2 3 4 5 6 7 8 9 10

Dedicated to dads everywhere…especially my own:
the late, great, Harvey Rosenberg. Love you, Dad.

TABLE OF CONTENTS

FOREWORD
By John A. Catsimatidis

When I bought WABC Radio, I bought a dream come true.

I grew up as an immigrant to this great country and listened to the old WABC Radio with enthusiasm and joy.

So when I had the opportunity to buy this station, I wanted to pay homage to its historical greatness as the premiere radio station in the United States. I wanted to restore it to its true greatness.

So what did I do? I searched out what made WABC Radio great. One name that stood out in music was Bruce Morrow, the legendary Cousin Brucie of rock and roll fame.

And one name stood out in talk radio—Sid Rosenberg of the renowned *Bernie & Sid in the Morning*.

What makes Sid a great talk radio host is what makes this book so exceptional. Sid is a genuine New York character.

He is smart, quick-witted, funny, well-informed, and courageous and forthright in his opinions. And I know where he gets his keen wit and street smarts from—his beloved mother who I've listened to on Sid's show. Most significantly, he is a wonderful and generous man who has overcome adversity and personal demons.

Whether it is drug abuse or a gambling addiction, he has confronted them and overcome them. He is a better man for it. He is a wonderful husband and father. He is a gifted voice of common sense in a world plagued by hypocritical, dishonest wokeism, which is a plague that undermines the human spirit and our wonderful country.

This book is Sid's story. His takes on government, politics, sports, popular culture, and medical health are well worth reading. His take on personal redemption is a lesson and model for all of us.

I am proud to say that Sid is an honored member of our WABC family. He is always worth listening to on the radio. And this book is well worth the reader's time and attention. The stories told and the lessons learned will only enrich readers' lives.

FOREWORD
By Bernard McGuirk

T he story of Sidney Rosenberg has all the twists, turns, highs, and lows of a Shakespearean play. Yes, at some points humiliation and failure (although not entirely self-inflicted), which eventually evolve into redemption and success.

Sid is an interesting character study. A walking paradox. On one hand, the embodiment of courage, determination, strength, confidence, resilience, persistence, and boundless energy.

On the other hand, at the same time, insecurity, anxiety off the charts, and a constant sense of foreboding lurking beneath all this exterior bravado.

I'll give you a little anecdote ladies and gentlemen: Back on December 8th, 2016, when we were both working for Imus, we were also doing the midday show from ten to noon, which would air right after the Imus show. Out of the blue, Sid says to me, "I'm dreading January third."

So, in other words, in Sid's mind, Christmas was out of the way, and he was already thinking about how horrible it's going to be to come back to Imus on January third. That's how much of a wreck Imus could turn Sid into.

I mention this just to give you an idea of the vulnerability of an otherwise muscled-out guy with a dark tan. A tan so dark by the way, I actually accused him of cultural appropriation. But it looks great on him.

He grew up in Brooklyn, a little Jewish kid, among Italians. Growing up in the wake of *Saturday Night Fever*, he wanted to be Italian so bad, which no doubt contributed to his insecurity, which today makes him a great radio talent. Both the confidence and the insecurity come out on the air.

He'll cry at the drop of a hat, which you'll no doubt be reading about in this book, *Sid-izens United*. The guy even cried when the actress and director Penny Marshall died. The broad from *Laverne & Shirley*. I mean, Shirley didn't even cry for God's sakes, but Sid Rosenberg was crying on the air. That's how complicated a character he is.

We first met over twenty years ago at WFAN Radio while working on the Imus show. Imus used to pit his employees against each other, and he did so with Sidney and myself. He'd always be pushing to see "Who's funnier? Who's better?" which eventually cumulated to a point where we actually fought in the ring.

It was an MSNBC televised three-round New York State amateur sanctioned bout. I came out victorious, but Sid fought with the heart of a lion and displayed sincere courage.

He was hurt, but he wouldn't give up. That's when I knew this guy Rosenberg was one tough son of a bitch. And he really is. Ironically, that fight cemented a lifelong bond we share to this day.

Years later when Sid was in South Florida, we'd stay in touch. He'd appear on the Imus show once in a while but only very infrequently. At that time, Sid was pretty much dead to Imus.

Then, as luck would have it, there was an opening at WABC Radio to fill the ten to twelve time slot, and Sid's name came up.

I wanted to work with Sid in the worst way. He's a natural talent. He's quick, he's funny, he's opinionated. Let's face it, this guy was born to be on the radio. I always thought we'd work together again after he left New York, and thankfully, we did.

He came back up, and we did a couple of shows together, and the powers that be knew immediately they had lighting in a bottle. They said, "Listen, this is radio magic right here. This is *Mike and the Mad Dog* stuff. This is *Hannity & Colmes, Curtis & Kuby.*"

So, they rightfully put Sid and me together. Thus, becoming the *Bernie & Sid Show.* Now we were off to the races. And once again, even without Imus, we were at odds.

We started in January of 2016, right in the middle of the presidential election. Sid was a Hillary supporter, and I was a Trump supporter. The constant back and forth bickering made for excellent radio.

I used to kid him and say, "Often in error, never in doubt." That's where his confidence and his appeal on the radio come into play. The attitude of, "I could never be wrong! You know I'm not wrong! Even though sometimes I may be wrong! But if I say it with enough sincerity and certitude it makes me sound like I'm right!" makes for very entertaining radio for anyone tuning in.

To Sid's credit, when Trump won, and he saw the great job Trump was doing, Sid acquiesced. He saw the light and came over to the right.

Another aspect of Sid's life you'll be reading about in this book is what a great family man Sid is. You're going to love reading about his connection with his dad, with his son, with his daughter, with his wife, Danielle, and also with you, the audience—in this case, the reader.

It is a fantastic life that he's had, which is still ongoing. It's still being written, folks. But Sid Rosenberg, to me, has been a blessing. I know you will enjoy this book.

To Sid, all my love. Thank you for being in my life.

INTRODUCTION

As many of my fans know, I was very close with both my parents, Naomi and Harvey, but especially my father, who was my Pop Warner football coach, my Little League baseball coach, and the man responsible for turning me on to sports as a little kid.

He took me to Met games, Giant games, and even Jets games when they were playing at Shea Stadium. As a kid, I loved the Jets and Broadway Joe Namath. One of my favorite childhood memories was when I won Mascot of the Week for the Jets in an A&S department store when I was eight years old. Out of thousands and thousands of applicants, they picked me, which guaranteed me a seat on the bench during a regular season Jets/Rams game, and gave me a chance to meet my hero, the aforementioned Broadway Joe, along with Emerson Boozer and all these other great Jet players.

At that time, Charley Winner was the coach of the Jets. He was the son-in-law of Weeb Ewbank. Weeb was the guy who coached the Jets to the Super Bowl III win over Don Shula and the Baltimore Colts. When Weeb retired, Charley took over as coach of the Jets. To be honest, Charley was a terrible coach, and the Jets were a terrible team; they were like 1–5 at that point, and the Jets, in their infinite wisdom, decided that little eight-year-old Sidney Ferris Rosenberg from Brooklyn could be a helpful distraction to a depressed fan base.

So, it's the middle of the week, and I'm all excited to be going to the game on Sunday, when out of nowhere, the Jets call my parents' house in Brooklyn (during dinner), and they pulled the invitation. That's right. The Jets pulled my invite! They told my father, "Listen we're sorry, but instead, we're going to give little Sidney a football signed by every player, we're going to give him a team jacket signed by Joe Namath, we're going to give him a bunch of Jets stuff all signed!" And they thought that was going to be okay with me?! I immediately started to scream and cry. I was eight years old, and I looked across the dinner table at my father and said: "Dad, what's the other team in New York that plays football?"

And he said, "Son, it's the team that I root for. It's the Giants."

I said, "I'm now a Giants Fan!" (And have been for the last forty-six years.)

That's when my father and I started going to Giants games together. We drove from New York to Tampa, Florida, to watch the Giants defeat the Buffalo Bills in Super Bowl XXV. We were very, very close. And he taught me a lot of lessons along the way, my father, but one of the big lessons he taught me as a child was persistence.

If my listeners know one thing about me, it's that I've been knocked down a lot. And honestly, a lot of times it's been my own fault. I mean, I've put myself in shitty situations because of different compulsions and addictions, and I've been told I'd never get up...but I always find a way to get up! Always! And usually, when I get up, I'm better than what I was in the last fight.

So, now I can take this all the way back to playing football at Kings Bay Football in Brooklyn, New York, as a little kid. I was a good player, a running back, and our team was the Redskins. My father was the coach. And one particular day we're playing the Steelers, and I knew all the kids on all the teams because they were all Brooklyn kids, neighborhood guys. I knew the good players, the bad players, the big guys, and the small ones, and the Steelers had this one kid who played defensive end. I think he was forty years old; I'm talking six foot four, 230 pounds, just a killer, so naturally, I was afraid to play the Steelers. I was still a little kid, a mama's boy, a good player, but I was still scared to death.

My buddy, Jerry Rocco, was our quarterback and a great young football player. In the backfield with me was this kid Michael Hart, but I was the go-to RB. Now it's time to play the Steelers, and my father is calling the plays and says to Jerry, "You're going to drop back three steps and pitch the ball to the right, to Sidney; Sidney, you're going to catch the pitch out and run." Now the killer, this "kid" is playing right defensive end. So, the play starts, Jerry takes the ball from center, moves back three steps, pitches me the football, and before I can even catch it, this damn guy, I swear to God, this guy was like "Mean" Joe Green. He absolutely belted me! I think I shit my pants to be honest with you. I got helped back up to my feet, went to the sidelines, missed a couple of plays, and came back into the game.

Now it's the second quarter, and my father says, "Here's the play. Jerry, you're going to drop back three steps. You're going to pitch the ball to Sidney. Sidney, you're going to catch the ball and run to the right." And I started to cry. "No Daddy, I'm not doing it. That guy almost killed me last time, don't make me call mommy! I swear to God, I'll call mommy. She doesn't want me to play anyway because of my asthma!" I was crying, I was angry. He says, "Son, stop it. Catch the ball and run." Eventually, he convinces me to do it.

Jerry drops back, pitches me the football, and as hard this "kid" hit me the first time, he hit me the second time. And now I really thought I died. I thought I died. I'm on the ground for a good five minutes. I think my body is convulsing. And I'm scared to death. I want to quit football forever. I get helped up, and back to the sideline I go.

Now, it's the fourth quarter, late in the game, and the score is close. My father is about to call a play. I'm looking at him and thinking, "Daddy, please don't do this to me again!" He says, "Here's the play! Jerry, you're going to drop back three steps and pitch the ball to Sidney. Sidney, you're going to catch the ball and run to the right!" You have to be kidding me! Now, I'm in shock. "Dad, you want me to die?! I mean, this guy has almost killed me twice...." But I didn't fight it. I didn't fight it. I said, "You know what? Screw it!"

Jerry drops back. He stops, pitches me the football. I make a move to my left, the "kid" from the Steelers makes a move to the left, and I spin to the right. And I'm gone. A sixty-five-yard touchdown. Now, I'm in the end zone. I won the game. I looked down the sideline to my father, he's about forty-five yards downfield, and I could see tears coming from his face like, "That's my son and I knew he could do it." And that's stayed with me forever. I mean, I almost got decapitated two times in a row, and there was no reason to believe that on the third effort anything would be different, no reason to think that would be the case. And yet, I scored the game-winning touchdown.

Thanks to my father's belief in me, that was the first time in my life that I was proud of myself for what I had accomplished. And that taught me a lesson that I've been living on and off for the last forty-six years.

Persistence.

Love you, Dad!

CHAPTER ONE

RESURRECTION-
BERG

When I got myself fired by 560 WQAM due to a DUI, it looked like my career was over. At least that's what I thought. At that point I had lost all my jobs in New York, and this was now the second job I had lost in Florida.

I was at a Japanese restaurant having dinner with my parents, my wife, Danielle, and my kids, when I got the call that I had been let go. I was previously told that my job was safe. The DUI didn't happen in a company car or on company time. The next day I even did a full show. In the end, however, none of that mattered, and I was shown the door.

At that time, I had a big fancy house in Boca, a couple of fancy cars, and two kids in private school. I was living pretty good. When I broke the bad news to Danielle, she started to cry, "Oh my God. What are we going to do?"

I remember thinking, *We're dead. What the fuck am I going to do? We're dead.* But I couldn't tell her that, so I said, "Listen, I'm not done. I know this is ugly. All the firings have been ugly. But I'm a young guy, I haven't killed anybody, I haven't raped anybody. We're going to figure this out. We'll get past this." Truth be told, in my heart of hearts, I didn't believe a word I was telling her. I honestly thought I was at the end of the road.

As luck would have it, I got a call from a guy named Steve Lapa who ran a small sports station in Pompano Beach, Florida—640 AM Sports. At this time there were four sports stations in South Florida: 790 The Ticket (they fired me), 560 WQAM (they fired me), 940 AM in Miami (they couldn't afford to pay me), and the smallest of them all, 640 AM.

Steve had tried to hire me years prior. He was a big Imus fan and loved New York radio. When he heard I was coming to Florida, he reached out, but the money he was offering was too low for me to take. This time, I might not have a choice.

Steve called and said, "I heard what happened. I think I might be able to help." We quickly setup a meeting.

We met at a bagel store in Boca Raton and got right down to business. He said, "I think you're great. I think you're phenomenal. I'm going to give you the morning show. I have a guy hosting the show now, but I'll get rid of him, and you'll get another chance."

I didn't mince words, "Steve, what can you pay me?"

"I can't promise you a lot, but I can give you something." He wrote the number on a napkin and passed it my way.

I took a look and almost died right there. I'm thinking, *Oh my god, how am I gonna do this?* Now, it was still a six-figure number, but it was a heck of a lot less than anything I'd ever made in radio. Ever. It was a number I knew was going to be very difficult to live on, but Steve went on to say that I'd have the opportunity to make more money by doing commercials and local appearances, and the number would go up, blah, blah, blah.

I called Danielle and she asked, "What's the number?" I told her, and needless to say, she wasn't thrilled. But I explained that this would lead to other opportunities to make money, and it would get me back in the game.

While I was at WFAN, never in a million years did I ever think I'd have to fall back on 640 AM in Pompano Beach for a much-needed career safety net, but what else was I going to do? For God's sake, I was still only in my forties. I had no choice. So, I took it.

Five days into the new gig and Karlos Dansby, a linebacker for the Dolphins, is a guest on the show. Karlos came on to voice his displeasure about the Dolphins cutting Chad "Ochocinco" Johnson over a domestic abuse charge. The reason this became a big deal was because that summer the Dolphins were the featured team on HBO's *Hard Knocks*, and they used the audio from my Karlos Dansby interview on the show.

At this point, most people in the radio business thought I was retired. That I was done. I was on 640 sports, the smallest of any station in South Florida, a station no one had even heard. Yet here I am making national news on HBO. It let everyone know that Sid Rosenberg was still around, still relevant, and still making news. I was also blessed to have the support of friends and colleagues like "The Greek," Joy Taylor, Victor Bermudez, Scott Kaplan, and Andy Slater in Miami. Here we go.

Things were going great at 640, and I was having fun on radio again, thanks in part to my producer Steve Zemach, and my board-op, Erik Lengyel. These two guys would have driven a car through a wall for me. And they did.

After a while, Joyce Kaufman, who was hosting a political show on our sister station 850AM would have me on as a guest, which opened the door for me to expand my show and platform outside of the world of sports and combine it into the world of politics. Steve Lapa was no fan of that decision. He said, "Listen, Sid, I hired you to do a sports show."

I said, "Steve, you hired me to be Sid Rosenberg. You hired the guy you watched on Imus. On Imus, I talked about everything: sports, politics, entertainment. That's the guy you hired. If you want me to sit here and jerk myself off and talk to Wes Welker for twenty minutes every Friday, you got the wrong guy. If you want someone who can do everything across the board, I'm the guy!"

Lapa responded, "You're so good. You're so talented, you're so enthusiastic about what you want to do. I'm going to give you a chance to sink or swim." Needless to say, we didn't sink. I owe a lot to Steve. I wouldn't be where I am today without his support and belief in me.

Owners of the station would soon go on to sell the station to The Alpha Group, and we moved from little Pompano Beach, Florida, to West Palm Beach and a much fancier studio. I was there for eight months before my contract was up, and the powers that be decided I was making way too much money. They wanted to move on. It's business and it happens. They just couldn't afford to pay me anymore. Once again, I was a free agent.

The good news is, four months prior to that, I got a call from Bernie at WABC in New York. He said, "Hey, you know, if you want to email Craig Schwab, the program director, they're willing to give us a couple of tryout shows to potentially work together."

I said, "You're kidding me." This was exciting news. I then had to go to my bosses in Florida to make sure this was okay for me to pursue. I don't think they were happy about that, which probably contributed to the reason why they didn't re-sign me. They had a feeling I was trying to get back to New York. They were right.

So, I did a couple of shows with Bernie in August and a couple in September. I thought we did great. I didn't think it could have gone any better. A few weeks go by, and I have yet to hear anything from the New York bosses. Were we a hit? Were we a flop?

It was around Thanksgiving that I called Bernie and said, "Well, I guess they didn't like us that much."

He said, "That's not true. They thought we were great. In fact, Geraldo Rivera's contract is up, and I don't think they're going to pay him. They might have an opening for us."

I sent Craig Schwab another email and said, "Listen, I don't know exactly what's going on with Geraldo, but I heard some rumors. Is there any way me and Bernie can do a couple more shows together?"

Craig responded, "Yes, come up in December."

We did two more shows and they loved them. They told us, "Let's see what happens with Geraldo, and we'll get back to you."

Now it's the end of December, and 640 shows me the door. I call Craig Schwab and say, "Well, I'm a free agent."

He says, "What are you talking about?"

I said, "They're not re-signing me. If you want me, I am ready, willing, and able to come back to New York."

Ever since I got the call from Bernie four months prior to my release, I was sending Schwab tapes of my 640 shows. I sent him tapes of my interviews with Chuck Todd, who was a regular guest every Friday, as well as interviews with six presidential candidates. This little sports station in Pompano Beach had all these monster personalities and politicians on the show because of who I was. I put that station on the map. So, when Craig listened to the tapes, he was like, "Wow, you've come a long way from the WFAN days. I think this will work on our station."

Now, at this point, unbeknownst to be, there was a power struggle inside the building because Don Imus didn't want them to bring me back. He wanted Mike Lupica to host the midday show. Imus was such a schmuck. You never knew from one day to the next if he loved or hated you.

Fortunately, Chad Lopez, the boss, loved me, and he over-ruled Imus. He said, "I know Sid has a very big loyal audience here in New York. I know Sid sells. He's young, he's exciting. Let's get Sid back!"

At the end of the day, my side came out victorious, thanks in large part to the lobbying and support from people like Chad, Pete Morgan, Curtis Sliwa, and my old producer, Jill Vitale, who all stuck up for me and Bernie.

Obviously, this never would have happened if it wasn't for the three years I spent at 640. Steve Lapa gave me one last chance at radio redemption, and I ran with it. With guys like Zemach and Lengyel at my side, I was able to take a rinky-dink station and turn it into something bigger than it was, and in doing so, it allowed me the opportunity to get back to where I belong, my hometown of New York.

Now that the power struggle was over, and it was written in stone that Sid Rosenberg was returning to town, it took Imus about fifteen minutes to fire Warner Wolf and bring me back on the show to do sports, which I did for the last year he was on the air. He knew it'd be a more entertaining show replacing Warner with me. He might be an asshole, but he's not stupid.

Just when things were really rolling along, Cumulus Media, our parent company, started selling off stations—big stations like WPLJ. We knew eventually it was going to be us too.

Now here comes billionaire John Catsimatidis into the picture. I didn't know him, and he didn't know me. I had no idea who he was. I wasn't in New York in 2013, when he unsuccessfully ran for the GOP mayoral nomination. I knew nothing about his businesses, even though I was shopping at Gristedes (a popular New York supermarket chain, which John owns) every day, which I still do now.

Fortunately, John and his wife, Margo, soon became loyal listeners to me and Bernie, and I'm proud to say that they're now among my biggest fans and cheerleaders and I love them. They are both incredibly loyal and supportive beyond words.

I was thrilled to already have done a contract with them once, and by the time you're reading this, I'll probably be on contract number two, and I don't see myself going anywhere for a long time, if ever; that's how much I love working for John and Margo. That's how good they are to me and my family.

The Catsimatidis family deserves a lot of credit for turning 77 WABC around. They brought in a lot of tremendous new talent, and the station is getting big ratings, led, of course, by me and Bernie, but also thanks to a weekday lineup of Brian Kilmeade, Greg Kelly, Lidia Curanaj, Rita Cosby, Frank Morano, and Dominic Carter. And a weekend lineup of Rudy Giuliani, Judge Jeanine, Larry Kudlow, Dick Morris, Bo Snerdley, and John Catsimatidis and his Sunday show, *Cats Roundtable*, and his weekday 5 p.m. show, *Cats at Night*.

It'd be an understatement for me to say it's a dream come true to be back in New York doing a job I love and was born to do. Every day I get a chance to entertain our listeners while discussing important matters of the day with great friends like Bernie, former Congressman Peter King, my childhood pal, Joe Tacopina, Rosanna Scotto, Rich Lowry, Rob Shuter, Dr. Nicole Saphier, Dr. Marc Siegel, Joyce Kaufman, Bo Dietl, and Bill O'Reilly, who does a fantastic job as a guest every Thursday at 8:40 a.m. on our show. He's even had Bernie and me on stage at his live show at the Paramount Theater in 2019. Over the years Bill has become a great friend. What a lot of people don't realize is just how generous a guy Bill really is. He spends an incredible amount of his time and energy dedicated to helping others. I know this from personal experience as Bill has been a tremendous help with my son's Spotlight Foundation.

I also have to mention the talented crew of people I get to work with every day like Lou Rufino, Justin Ellick, Luke

Lograno, Frankie Diez, Christina Aversa, Deb Valentine, Gabby Lopez, and my Program Director, Matt Meany. It's an exciting time in my life, and I'm fortunate enough to get to share it with my family, my friends, and my fans.

But stay tuned, folks. Because, like an Italian fella from Hoboken once said, "The best is yet to come."

CHAPTER TWO

SIDNEY-WOOD

Being in movies or on TV was never a main goal of mine. In fact, until recently, the only acting I'd ever done was when I was a kid starring in my camp plays. My first big role was in *Bye Bye Birdie* where I played Albert (I think Dick Van Dyke played that role in the movie and on Broadway). People told me I did a pretty good job, but it wasn't like Warner Bros. was offering little Sidney Rosenberg from Brooklyn a three-picture deal and screen time with Farrah Fawcett.

So, any notion of a budding acting career was put on the back burner, which is why it came as a surprise when, in the early 2000s, while I was working at WFAN, a call came into the newsroom from somebody saying, "Hey Sid, you got a call from Los Angeles."

I hopped on the phone. "Hi this is Sid Rosenberg."

A girl on the other end said, "Hello, this is Christine from DreamWorks."

"DreamWorks? Steven Spielberg's DreamWorks?" I said, half stunned.

"Yeah, this is Christine from DreamWorks. You may not know this but Jerry Seinfeld is a very big fan of yours."

"No, I didn't know that," I said.

At that time, I knew Jerry Seinfeld was an avid WFAN listener. I knew he was very good friends with Steve Somers, a New York sports radio legend, and I knew he loved the Mets, but I had no idea Jerry Seinfeld even knew who I was let alone being a "big fan" of mine.

"He's a big fan and he's making a movie. It's an animated film called *Bee Movie*, and he thinks there's a part in it that would be perfect for you. He loves your comic delivery. He loves the Brooklyn voice and your whole approach, and he thinks you would be perfect."

Now completely stunned, I could only muster up a "He does?" response.

"Yeah, he does. He's going to be at a recording studio in midtown Manhattan, if you'd like to meet him and read for the part."

This was the ultimate no-brainer. Meet Jerry Seinfeld? Read for a movie part? "OF COURSE!"

Now I go to meet Jerry Seinfeld at this recording studio and read for the part of a hornet. After about three hours, Jerry came over to me and said, "Sid, that's exactly what I envisioned for this character; your voice, your delivery, perfect!"

I thought, Holy shit. I made the movie!

He said, "You were great!" and that was that.

I walked out of there thinking. I was there for three hours, I just got paid double union scale, Seinfeld was filled with compliments, I got this!

Now, the movie starts to come out, and I'm checking the IMDB, looking for my beautiful Sid Rosenberg credit (the first of many more credits to come), but as I searched and searched, I found nothing. At this point in the story if you've ever seen *Bee Movie* and are trying to recall a hornet with a strong Brooklyn accent, well you can stop that now. You haven't. Turns out I was just another casualty of the cutting room floor. They never used it. I was crushed. End of my acting career, right?

Not so fast…one end turns into a *Gravesend.*

About two years ago, a buddy of mine from my South Florida radio days, Larry Milian, gives me a call in New York and says, "Have you ever heard of the show *Gravesend?*"

I said, "No, never heard of it."

Larry goes on to explain that the show is shot in Brooklyn, and the creator and lead actor, William DeMeo, who is also the writer and director, is a fan of mine and wants to talk. I said, "Sure," and we exchanged numbers. William called me a bunch of times, but I was always busy and never picked up, because, honestly, I never really took it seriously. But sure enough, through persistence, one day he finally got through to me, and we had a great conversation.

I invited him down to the studio to hop on the air with me and Bernard and let him promote *Gravesend*. While he was there, he kept mentioning that I'd be perfect for his show. "You got the look, you're Brooklyn. Who's more Brooklyn than you? Nobody! I can see it already."

With me, a little sweet talking can get you a long way. So, I eventually said, "Let's do it."

Now, I arrive at a park in Miami Beach to start filming. It was early in the morning on a Friday, and there was a big trailer, and there were two doors with the names of our fictional characters. Andrew Dice Clay plays Rinaldo, so on one door there's "Rinaldo," and on the other door there were the names "Dave" (which was the name of my character, Dave Busco) and my buddy Chris Mormando, who plays the role of Gaetano.

I've finally arrived. I've got a trailer. I've got food in there. I've got drinks in there. I've got a closet to hang my clothes, people to iron my pants and iron my shirt, makeup comes in. I'm bald but hair people would've come in if needed. Our lunch and breakfast were served in there. And it's where I hung out between scenes. I had a legitimate movie trailer. Pretty damn cool.

Outside of that I gotta tell you, it's a lot of standing around while they reshoot the same scene for what feels like a hundred times. After the first two takes, I'm thinking, This is great. This is perfect. Done. But, no, no, no. You shoot over and over again. Unlike radio, where you're on and that's it—you got four hours, keep talking—on a TV and movie set, there's a ridiculous amount of down time. Reshoot, reshoot, reshoot, with breaks in between where the director might change some things, and the writer might add or delete some things. I loved the atmosphere of being on a legit set, I loved the trailer, but it's a lot of waiting, almost the entire day. But, hey, there are worse ways to make a living.

Fortunately, this particular acting opportunity came to fruition, and yours truly did not end up on the cutting room floor. I'd already filmed three or four scenes in Miami with Andrew Dice Clay, William DeMeo, Peter Gaudio, Vic Dibitetto, and Leo Rossi, and had more scenes lined up with Armand Assante in Brooklyn and Miami over the next couple of months, and that was really my first foray into acting on a legit TV show.

Since then, I've been offered two movie roles. One of them from Danny A. (Danny Abeckaser) who is a big-time guy in the business. He's great friends with DiCaprio and made a bunch of movies. He's been in *The Irishman* and *The Wolf of Wall Street*. A very impressive guy who now makes his own movies, stars in them, writes and directs them. I went to one of his movie premieres a few months ago in New York and he said, "Man, you really do look the role." He's making a movie about the former Gambino gangster Roy DeMeo and his notorious hangout spot the Gemini Lounge, which was a bar in Brooklyn where the mob would cut up bodies. So, he gave me a role in the movie as, you guessed it, another mobster. I'm playing DeMeo's cousin, Joe "Dracula" Guglielmo, alongside many talented actors such as Robert Davi, Emile Hirsch, Lucy Hale, and Jake Cannavale.

Now, I have *Gravesend*, which is still shooting. I start the Danny A. movie in October, and now a third film role has come my way. A movie called *The Tank Job*, spearheaded by CNBC's Ron Insana, which is about the 1963 near stock market crash in Bayonne, New Jersey, and he's got me playing the role of Tino De Angelis who pulled off a Bernie Madoff-like scheme known as the "Salad Oil scandal."

So those are three serious acting roles: one TV series that's very successful on Amazon Prime, and two legitimate movies that are about to film. My love and appreciation to William DeMeo for giving me my first opportunity on TV and to Danny A, for giving me my first opportunity in movies. Not bad for a kid from Brooklyn.

Perception VS Reality?

Over the span of my career, I've interviewed four presidents and nearly every major sports figure. Tiger Woods was quiet, but he wasn't a dick. Shaquille O'Neal was quiet, but he wasn't a dick. Michael Jordan wasn't a dick. I've interviewed the biggest and the best in sports, politics, and entertainment, and I can't think of more than one or two people where I was like, Wow, I truly hate that person. That person was a real dick!

Which is why I had some trepidation when I first got the gig on *Gravesend* and learned I'd be working closely with Andrew Dice Clay. I had heard from more than a few people that he could be, well, a bit of a dick. So, I arrive on set, and the first scene I do is with Dice. Dice and William DeMeo are the two stars, and they're walking down the beach. I play Dice's bodyguard, so I've got an umbrella, which I'm holding for Dice. Chris Mormando is holding another umbrella for DeMeo, and we're walking down the beach on an eighty-degree, sunny, windy day in Miami in April.

Before the scene starts, I walk over to Dice to shake his hand, and very abruptly he moves away and turns around. I say to myself, Holy shit. What a dick! What the hell was that? Then I see him talking to William DeMeo. I walk away with Chris Mormando, thinking, Oh my god, I gotta shoot like nine hours working with this guy today. Here we go.

About two minutes later Dice comes walking over and he goes, "Listen man, it's the COVID. I freak out over COVID. I don't know what to do, I don't want to get sick, I don't really know who you are, don't take it personally, because I'm like that with everybody. I'm freaked out over the COVID. Don't get upset."

And I'm like, "Okay, no problem. I totally get it."

We were together for the next seven hours, taping scenes inside a car, on a tennis court, on the beach probably three or four scenes in all. And then we shot again two days later inside an old Miami hotel where I was playing billiards, and he was sitting outside on the porch, and he could not have been nicer. He was great to work with and kept giving me pointers, telling me what to say, what not to say, really showing me the ropes. The guy was an absolute champ.

The truth is most of the people you watch on TV or in movies (particularly mob movies) are regular guys who couldn't be more different or distant from their on-screen personas. For instance, I know the whole *Sopranos* cast very well. I knew Jimmy before he died. Steven Van Zandt is a good personal friend, as is Steve Schirripa. They're regular guys who could be your cousin, your uncle, your buddy, who don't come off as characters to necessarily be afraid of or intimidated by.

However, the guys who are extras or consultants on some of these shows, like Chuck Zito and his friend Johnny, will scare the shit out of you in real life. Usually though, the stars of these shows or movies, like De Niro, Pesci, Pacino, have long gray hair, talk a heck of a lot slower, and are really painfully shy. I mean you can never imagine the real Joe Pesci actually taking Sharon Stone's head and shoving it down towards his penis outside of a movie like *Casino*. You would never imagine that in a million years. That's why it's called acting, folks.

Note To Celebrities: STFU

They say opinions are like assholes: everyone's got one. Unfortunately, this includes asshole celebrities.

With elections looming, political debates, and never-ending pleas for financial contributions, which have invaded and bombarded the homes and lives of any person who isn't lucky enough to live under a rock, one aspect of the political season never fails to rear its ugly and unwelcome head: the unavoidable appearance of celebrity opinions and endorsements.

Every other November, actors, musicians, pop culture icons, athletes, and other public figures love to come out of the woodwork and begin spouting about how you would be an idiot if you didn't vote for their candidate. The idea of actors, singers, and athletes talking down to American voters like they are idiots is not only offensive but dangerous. Unfortunately, the American people are all too familiar with "influencers" attempting to push their agendas whenever it's time to cast a ballot.

Most irritating of all is the fact that many of these celebrities act like they are pushing a political agenda for the common American without having any idea what that lifestyle is like. Actresses such as airhead Gwyneth Paltrow love to preach about how the candidates or policies they are supporting are good for America, but this is the same woman who said in an interview that she "couldn't live" without her $25,000 custom bookshelf. Talk about out-of-touch.

American voters still possess the best tool for filtering celebrities' opinions: don't listen to them! Don't take political advice from a person who has no relative understanding of your life. Do your research, read your ballot, and vote for the candidate that you believe has your best interests at heart. It's unfortunate that so few of us do.

Look, I have friends who won't see a De Niro movie. I think that's a bit ridiculous. Same goes for Barbra Streisand. They'll never go to another concert. I don't take it that far. I just don't. Doesn't mean I don't hate their politics. I just attempt to not pay attention to them. I'm not about to deprive myself of a good movie or TV show because I don't like a celebrity's views on certain topics. But I do hate it, and I get why others do as well.

If you're an actor, and you want as many people as possible to come to the theater, why polarize any bit of your audience? Me? I don't have a choice, I'm on radio. That's my job. My job is to be polarizing. My job is to be opinionated and talk about these things, politics especially, but if you don't have to do it, why would you?

It gets very visceral. I mean, it's one thing to say, "I don't really like Donald Trump." I can live with that, but as De Niro said, "I want to bash his brains in!" Really? What about Joe Biden, who's a first-class schmuck and has no idea what he's doing? Do you want to punch Joe Biden across the face? I don't care if these people have opinions. They're allowed. I have an opinion, you've got an opinion, but the visceral reaction, the way they talk about it just turns people off.

From a financial aspect, it's absurd to push away any part of your audience. These are the folks who have airtime every day on television that millions of Americans watch, and there's no reason for them to be that hateful. Sure, have an opinion. If there's a big story, give your thoughts: "Hey, I'm not happy about this. I'm happy about that." Whatever, but to have that type of bias (for my money, Joy Behar is the absolute worst!) every day, as an actor or a television star, I don't get it.

COVID the Destroyer?

The COVID-19 pandemic has had an impact on nearly all aspects of our lives, and the film industry is no exception. It's estimated that the US box office alone has lost an estimated $5 billion since the virus hit.

Movie theaters are by nature a high-risk environment, as they often pack hundreds of people into a small space together for extended periods of time, making them less than ideal destinations for a night out with the family.

So how have businesses like movie theater chains and film production companies adjusted to these unprecedented times? Movie theaters have arguably been hit the hardest, and several major chains have been forced to close down permanently.

Even AMC, which fortunately had a very good run with the new Spider-Man movie, came very close to having to file for bankruptcy. Some smaller chains and independent theaters have allowed small groups of people to book private screenings in an attempt to earn some money. Several states have announced support for a socially distanced reopening of theaters, but with distribution companies favoring streaming services for the release of new films, combined with most film-goers still wary of the virus, makes you wonder whether it will ever get back to pre-COVID numbers.... Here's a hint. It will never be the same again. Never.

Before COVID, my family and I loved going to the movies. We'd make a night out of it. We were members of the IPIC theaters and would often frequent the one at the South Street Seaport close to where we used to live on Hanover Square by Wall Street. (By the way, it's very expensive.) They have chairs that lay down like beds, they give you blankets and pillows, all the food you want, all the alcohol you want, all the candy you want, delivered right to your seat. It was a lap of luxury.

We'd do the same thing down in South Florida. We were members of the IPIC theater in Boca Raton. We are a big movie family. We watch them at home or in the theaters, it's one of our passions, but unfortunately, for the better part of a year and a half, even though theaters are open, we've yet to see the inside of one. My family is still kind of freaked out and won't go. I would go, but it's a major void because that was something we all did together on a regular basis.

Sure, you can basically watch everything from the comfort of your couch, especially now with all the streaming services, but, after a while, you just want to get out of your house. People are doing everything from home: work from home, eat from home, and now watching movies from home. Because of the virus we've been deprived of another avenue of activity that would involve walking out the front door.

Even if I could see every new movie released from the comfort of my own home, I'd rather go to a theater and make a night of it. Get some fresh air, candy, and all that type of stuff. The point is you need to get out!

Unfortunately, I think it'll be increasingly difficult for a lot of these theaters to stay in business. The successful ones will need to be in big, booming cities with big audiences, or they're not going to make it. These little mom-and-pop theaters in Clarksville, Tennessee, or La Crosse, Wisconsin, are going to be in trouble, while a theater in a high traffic area like Times Square has a better chance of survival.

Drive-in theaters? It's a little bit of a pain in the ass, to be honest. I've gone to a drive-in theater since COVID, and it was a lot of fun, but I'm not sure they're going to start building these things in mass numbers. As of October 2019, only 305 drive-in theaters remained in the US, according to the United Drive-In Theatre Owner Association (UDITOA). The major problem is real estate: a five-hundred-car drive-in requires about ten to fourteen acres. You also need low ambient light and graded ramps for proper sight lines. According to UDITOA, there is a mathematical formula that dictates the ideal angle and distance between the screen and projection booth. So, it's cute. It's a good idea. It's a good shtick. I enjoyed it. But don't expect to be seeing a drive-in theater at a local community near you.

Prediction: I think what you're going to be seeing in the immediate future are companies making bigger flat screen TVs. You'll see eighty inches, one hundred inches, or 120 inches, and they'll make them more affordable so regular folks can buy them. It'll no longer be a situation where you need to be Gwyneth Paltrow with a private screening room in a Hamptons mansion to enjoy an in-home theater experience.

SID-IZEN SOLUTION

Let me say this: just because there's a significant decline in movie theaters across the country doesn't mean there's a decline in the quality of movie making.

These streaming services are doing great. Absolutely great. Clearly people are still interested in good content, whether it's a movie or a TV show or series. So, I don't think the movie industry is a bygone era. I just think that it's cheaper to stay home. It got very expensive to go to the movies. A night at the theater for me and my family was over a hundred dollars. However, it's vitally important to support the American entertainment industry in any way possible. Go to movies if you can afford it.

We make a lot of things in this country. We don't make everything the best. That's just the bottom line. But there are certain things we do here that no other country can compete with. Entertainment is one of those areas. TV, movies, theater, no one does it as well as the United States.

So, of course some of these actors piss us off, I get it. You hate their politics and blah, blah, blah. But you have to try to find a way to be an adult and separate the two. Let De Niro yell and scream and make a fool out of himself. Don't let it bother you. But if he's in a new mob movie with Joe Pesci, Al Pacino, and Bo Dietl, you go see it. I don't care if it's in a theater or in the comfort of your own home.

We do entertainment very well in this country; whether it's a weekly sitcom, series, or a movie. Personally, I'm on the streaming services every night. I have at least five or six shows I watch every week. So, I would hope that the passion continues in America, whether it's going out to a theater once a month or just staying home.

Let's keep the United States the number one exporter of global entertainment.

CHAPTER THREE

SIDNESS = FITNESS

I f you asked me thirty years ago what my workout routine was like, you'd probably get an answer that resembles something like this:

Monday: Cardio.
Tuesday: Weightlifting.
Wednesday: Ten-year break.

These days, working out and staying fit are a huge part of my life. If I don't work out for a couple days, I'll get in a bad mood. That's just the way it is. I need the action. I need the activity.

When I had my difficulties down in Florida and was getting fired from jobs, outside of my family, going to the gym was my savior, and it served as a two-prime purpose for me. It certainly made me look better. Anyone who knows me might tell you I can be a bit narcissistic, and I like to look good in clothes, so the physical aspect is essential. But what I came to realize was that the mental side was just as important, even bigger, and continues to be all these years later.

Half the battle is mental. Making the decision to do it and committing to do it ain't easy. When I first started working out in a serious way, it was painful. I was always sore. I mean always sore. I was quickly winded. I couldn't lose any weight. Sometimes I was embarrassed to go to the gym because I would struggle with a ten-pound dumbbell while standing next to guys using sixty, seventy, eighty pounds. But I had persistence and kept going and kept getting stronger and feeling better about myself to a point where going to the gym and working out became second nature.

Now, at least twice a week, somebody in the gym will walk up to me and say, "What do you charge?"

In the beginning I was like, "Charge for what?"

"Well, you're obviously a trainer," they'd say.

I hate breaking the shocking news to them, but it's proof that if you have a workout plan and stick to it, people will start seeing the results and think, "Hey, this guy knows what he's doing. I'm going to hire him." Also, having a great tan doesn't hurt.

Now you're asking yourself, "Sid, how does working out help you mentally just as much as it does physically? Would you happen to have five specific examples?"

Well, you've come to the right place. In fact, I do.

Let's break it down:

1. Help for Depression and Anxiety

Exercise is a scientifically proven mood booster, decreasing symptoms of both depression and anxiety. Physical activity kicks up endorphin levels, the body's famous "feel good" chemical produced by the brain and spinal cord that produces feelings of happiness and euphoria (same feeling when Scott Norwood missed the game-ending field goal in Super Bowl XXV).

Even just moderate exercise throughout the week can improve depression and anxiety, so much so that some doctors recommend trying out an exercise regimen for these conditions before turning to medication options.

2. Decreased Stress

Another mental benefit of exercise is reduced stress levels—something that can make us all happier. Increasing your heart rate can actually reverse stress-induced brain damage by stimulating the production of neurohormones like norepinephrine, which not only improve cognition and mood but improve thinking clouded by stressful events. Exercise also forces the body's central and sympathetic nervous systems to communicate with one another, improving the body's overall ability to respond to stress.

3. Increased Self-Esteem and Self-Confidence

From improving endurance to losing weight and increasing muscle tone, there's no shortage of physical achievements that come about from regular exercise. All those achievements add up to a shit ton of self-esteem and all the confidence that comes with it.

You may not set out for better-fitting clothes, a slimmer physique, and the ability to climb a hill without getting winded. Oftentimes, it happens before you even realize it. Those are just some of the many benefits of physical activity that boost your body, mind, and spirit.

4. Better Sleep

If you have trouble getting to sleep on your My Pillow, exercise can help with that too. Physical activity increases body temperature, which can have calming effects on the mind, leading to less sheep-counting and more shut-eye. Exercise also helps regulate your circadian rhythm, our body's built-in alarm clock that controls when we feel tired and when we feel alert.

5. Food for Thought

From building intelligence to strengthening memory, exercise boosts brainpower in a number of ways. Studies on mice and humans indicate that cardiovascular exercise creates new brain cells, a process called neurogenesis, and improves overall brain performance. It also prevents cognitive decline and memory loss by strengthening the hippocampus, the part of the brain responsible for memory and learning. Studies also prove that physical activity boosts creativity and mental energy. So, if you're in need of inspiration, your big idea could be a run through Central Park away.

✪　✪　✪

Let me tell you, twenty years ago, I wasn't a fan of how I looked, especially the way I looked on TV. So, when Danielle and I moved to Chelsea around 2003, I joined the Chelsea Piers gym. After a while I started to put on a little bit of muscle, and the confidence followed.

I started to feel pretty good about myself. So good in fact, I would go on the air with Bernard, and we would exchange so many insulting barbs back and forth that it eventually resulted in one of the most famous celebrity fights in radio history.

It was billed as "Fear at the Pier." October of 2003, Bernie and I would duke it out at Chelsea Piers. I was training hard, putting on some size and getting into shape. Unfortunately for me, Bernie was always in great shape. He's a decade older than me, but back then it didn't matter; he was still a young guy.

I also need to mention that about three months before the fight, my wife and I decided to leave Chelsea, and we bought a house in Tenafly, New Jersey. There was so much going on at that time that I stopped training. Big. F'n. Mistake.

So, as you can imagine, I got walloped in those three rounds by Bernard, to the point where they had to call the fight. Lee Davis, who previously worked with Howard Stern, was the big boss at WFAN back in 2003. He stopped the fight because he was scared I was going to get seriously hurt and sue CBS. Although I never fell and hit the canvas (in tribute to *Raging Bull*: "I never went down, Bernie. You never got me down."), I did take a pretty good beating. At least Bernie didn't leave the ring unscathed. He had a concussion and a bloody nose. So, let the record show that Sid "The Kid" got his shots in too.

It would be about a year later when I started to take working out seriously again. My agent at the time, Mark Lepselter, who also represented Tiki Barber, Joe Benigno, and Lawrence Taylor, was working out with a guy named Joe Carini, and Mark introduced us.

Joe had this real old school, bad ass gym in Jersey. You'd see all these big guys doing crazy exercises like hooking up ropes to cars and seeing how far they could drag them. Crazy cool shit. I would make an hour trip at like four in the morning, before Imus, to work out with Carini and that was when I started to really put on some size and make working out a permanent part of my life.

Even when I got fired by WFAN in 2005 and went down to south Florida for what turned out to be eleven years and jobs at three radio stations, I took my workout routine very seriously. I had such a new physique that by the time I got back to New York in 2016, most people who hadn't seen me since I left WFAN barely recognized me. "Whoa, you put some size on, Sid. You look great." I did feel great. Mentally and physically.

I can proudly tell you that six years later, I'm probably twice as big. I've been training with Peter Gaudio, a great actor who is also in the Amazon Prime series *Gravesend* with me. He's by far the most muscular and fit sixty-two-year-old guy I've ever seen in my life.

At the moment, I'm definitely in the best shape I've ever been in, which has kind of become part of my persona. I finally like how I look on TV. My jackets are tight, I dress very well, thanks to beautiful clothes by Joseph Abboud, and all that goes into the Sid Rosenberg you know and love today.

I credit my physical appearance as a big reason, if not the main reason, why I find myself getting acting gigs. If I looked like I did back in 2001 at WFAN, I wouldn't be in these shows and movies. I just wouldn't be. I play a bodyguard in one role and a tough Italian guy in another.

So, while I say working out and keeping fit is for my mental and physical health (which it is), it also has absolutely made a difference in my career. One hundred percent, all my acting gigs, right now, are the result of working out and the physical benefits it's produced for me. It's also the reason why I was fortunate to land the February 2022 cover of *FLG* magazine. Thanks to Vikki Press and Michael Goldman for their hard work on making that a success.

Now you're asking yourself, "Sid, how does working out help you physically just as much as it does mentally? Would you happen to have five specific examples?"

Well, you've come to the right place. In fact, I do.

Let's break it down:

1. Weight Management

Looking to get to or stay at a healthy weight? Both diet and physical activity play a critical role in maintaining a healthy body weight, losing excess body weight, or maintaining successful weight loss. You gain weight when you consume more calories through eating and drinking than the amount of calories you burn, including those burned during physical activity. It's important to balance calories. When it comes to weight management, people vary greatly in how much physical activity they need. You may need to be more active than others to reach or maintain a healthy weight.

To maintain your weight: work your way up to 150 minutes a week of moderate-intensity aerobic activity (for example, thirty minutes a day, five days a week). Strong scientific evidence shows that physical activity can help you maintain your weight over time. However, the exact amount of physical activity needed to do this is not clear since it varies greatly from person to person. It's possible that you may need to do more than 150 minutes of moderate-intensity activity a week to maintain your weight.

To lose weight and keep it off: you will need a high amount of physical activity unless you adjust your diet and reduce the amount of calories you're eating and drinking. Getting to and staying at a healthy weight requires both regular physical activity and a healthy eating plan.

2. Reduce Your Health Risk

Cardiovascular Disease

Heart disease and stroke are two of the leading causes of death in the United States. Following the recommendations and getting at least 150 minutes a week of moderate-intensity aerobic activity can put you at a lower risk for these diseases.

You can reduce your risk even further with more physical activity. Regular physical activity can also lower your blood pressure and improve your cholesterol levels.

Type 2 Diabetes and Metabolic Syndrome

Regular physical activity can reduce your risk of developing type 2 diabetes and metabolic syndrome. Metabolic syndrome is some combination of too much fat around the waist, high blood pressure, low high-density lipoprotein (HDL) cholesterol, high triglycerides, or high blood sugar. People start to see benefits at levels of physical activity below the recommended 150 minutes a week. Additional amounts of physical activity seem to lower risk even more.

Some Cancers

Being physically active lowers your risk for developing several commonly occurring cancers. Research shows that adults who participate in greater amounts of physical activity have reduced risks of developing cancers of the:

> Bladder
> Breast
> Colon (proximal and distal)
> Endometrium
> Esophagus (adenocarcinoma)
> Kidney
> Lung
> Stomach (cardia and non-cardia adenocarcinoma)

Improve your quality of life. If you are a cancer survivor, research shows that getting regular physical activity not only helps give you a better quality of life, but also improves your physical fitness.

3. Strengthen Your Bones and Muscles

As you age, it's important to protect your bones, joints, and muscles—they support your body and help you move. Keeping bones, joints, and muscles healthy can help ensure you're able to do your daily activities and be physically active.

Doing aerobics, muscle-strengthening, and bone-strengthening physical activity at a moderately intense level can slow the loss of bone density that comes with age. Hip fracture is a serious health condition that can have life-changing negative effects, especially if you're an older adult. Physically active people have a lower risk of hip fracture than inactive people.

Among older adults, physical activity also reduces the risk of falling and injuries from falls. Physical activity programs that include more than one type of physical activity are most successful at reducing falls and fall-related injuries.

Different types of physical activity include aerobic, muscle strengthening, and balance physical activities. Also, weight bearing activities such as running, brisk walking, jumping jacks, and strength training produce a force on the bones. These activities can help promote bone growth and bone strength and reduce the risk of fall-related injuries and fractures.

Regular physical activity helps with arthritis and other rheumatic conditions affecting the joints. Doing 150 minutes a week of moderate-intensity aerobic physical activity, if able, plus muscle-strengthening activity improves your ability to manage pain and do everyday tasks and improves quality of life.

Build strong, healthy muscles. Muscle-strengthening activities like lifting weights can help you increase or maintain your muscle mass and strength. This is important for older adults who experience reduced muscle mass and muscle strength with aging. Slowly increasing the amount of weight and number of repetitions you do as part of muscle strengthening activities will give you even more benefits, no matter your age.

4. Improve Your Ability to Do Daily Activities and Prevent Falls

A functional limitation is a loss of the ability to do everyday activities such as climbing stairs, grocery shopping, or playing with your grandchildren.

How does this relate to physical activity? If you're a physically active middle-aged or older adult, you have a lower risk of functional limitations than people who are inactive.

For older adults, multicomponent physical activity is important to improve physical function and decrease the risk of falls or injury from a fall. Multicomponent physical activity is physical activity that includes more than one type of physical activity, such as aerobic, muscle strengthening, and balance training. Multicomponent physical activity can be done at home or in a community setting as part of a structured program.

5. Increase Your Chances of Living Longer

Science shows that physical activity can reduce your risk of dying early from leading causes of death, like heart disease and some cancers. This is remarkable in two ways:

Only a few lifestyle choices have as large an impact on your health as physical activity. People who are physically active for about 150 minutes a week have a 33 percent lower risk of all-cause mortality than those who are physically inactive.

You don't have to do high amounts of activity or vigorous-intensity activity to reduce your risk of premature death. Benefits start to accumulate with any amount of moderate or vigorous-intensity physical activity.

Look, I tell people you need to do three things: cardio, weightlifting, and supplements. Don't forget supplements—the right ones.

I think if you do two of those three, you're not going to get nearly the same results. If you do one or zero of those three, you're not going to get anything. If you want the ultimate results, it's got to be cardio, weightlifting, and supplements.

First Things First: Cardio

Intensity is key. As intensity rises, more calories get burned. That's why high-intensity interval workouts are a smart choice for getting shredded while maintaining (or even gaining) muscle.

Here are the expert-approved top ten types of cardio to help you lose weight faster and show results sooner:

1. Sprinting

Sprints outside, on a treadmill, or even up stairs or bleachers are a great way to burn the most calories in the least amount of time. No equipment is really necessary, and you can do these workouts just about anywhere. Sprinting is simple, and it burns huge amounts of calories. When looking to shed weight, it tops the list. While steady-state running or jogging burns plenty of calories, increasing your speed and intensity will really pay off.

2. *High-Intensity Interval Training (HIIT)*

HIIT gives you a well-rounded workout while burning a ton of fat and calories. HIIT workouts can vary greatly, from five hundred calories per hour to 1500-plus calories per hour for a 180-pound man. HIIT workouts are great because of the intensity of each exercise as well as the variation of exercises and reps. Pair any body weight movement with a weighted movement and a traditional cardio element, and you have the perfect recipe for an amazing fat-burner.

3. *Rowing*

It's a great way to incorporate the upper and lower body in a relatively low-stress manner on your joints and ligaments. It's also a great way to work the posterior chain. Following a moderate pace on the rowing machine can burn upwards of eight hundred calories per hour for a 180-pound guy, but increasing the intensity with short sprints will get that number well over one thousand calories per hour very quickly.

4. Swimming

Swimming is a total-body workout that starts the second you begin treading water. You're essentially fighting gravity, so your muscles are working extra hard to keep you afloat without getting a break until you're out of the water. In fact, with just one minute of fast swimming, you'll burn fourteen calories.

5. Jumping Rope

There's a reason the jump rope is a mainstay in a boxer's training regimen: it's cheap, easy to do, increases foot speed, and burns a ton of calories. Think of your favorite boxers, wrestlers, and fighters. They all jump rope.

Jumping rope not only enhances your footwork, shoulder strength, and coordination, but also simulates sprinting, allowing you to burn as much as five hundred calories in just thirty minutes.

6. Stair Climber

A stair climber offers another popular way to burn fat and calories, but only about five hundred to six hundred calories for a 180-pound man at a moderate pace. Because of the higher leg lift involved, climbing stairs uses significantly more muscles than just walking, strengthening your legs in a functional way.

The primary drawback: stair climbers can put a lot of weight and pressure on your joints, so it can be difficult for people with bad knees.

7. Running (Moderate Pace)

Running at a steady, moderate pace is a sure way to burn fat and calories, but it's not the most economical way to build or even maintain muscle. By the numbers, a 180-pound man can burn about 940 calories in an hour while running 8.5-minute-per-mile pace, or 7 miles per hour on the treadmill for an hour.

This would be a nice, long run to do every couple of weeks to keep up your aerobic capacity, but it involves a lot of mileage for the time and effort put in. The cons: running at this pace can also break down muscle and subject your body to lots of pounding. If you're looking to add in a long run every once in a while, by all means do so, just opt for trails or softer surfaces than cement and blacktop.

8. Elliptical

These machines were originally designed to minimize impact on the knees and hips while still allowing for a great workout because the impact is quite low. But the calorie-burning effect isn't as great as other cardio machines like treadmills and StairMasters.

However, the elliptical machine can be an excellent way to burn calories without wearing out your joints.

While the average 180-pound man may only burn close to five hundred to six hundred calories per hour if he's going at an above-moderate pace, you can get even more out of it by switching up the intensity, speed, and resistance. Now, on to my personal favorite if you couldn't tell:

9. *Weightlifting*

First Steps for First-Time Lifters

So, where's a newbie iron slinger to start? It can be as simple as mastering a few basic lifts. But before you grab a set of thirty-pounders, it's important to nail down proper form and safe technique with moderate weights. You'll know you're at a solid starting weight if you feel like you have two more reps left in you after the prescribed five to six.

Of the strength exercises below, I'd suggest working one or two into your training session once per week. You could choose a new one each day, or if you're opting for two, go with one that focuses on the upper body and one on lower body. Now let's get ready to lift!

Hex Bar Dead Lift

How to: Start standing tall, inside of the hex bar with feet hip-width apart.

a) Push your hips back as far as possible while still maintaining a vertical shin position. Bend your knees until you can grab the bar with both hands.

b) With your knees slightly bent, back flat, and abs tight, stand straight up, engaging your glutes.

c) Hinge at the hips again and lower your chest back down—maintain that flat back—until the weight lightly touches the floor.

d) Stand again and repeat. At the end, slowly lower the bar back to the ground, just as you did to pick it up.

Form focus: Keep your chest up and maintain a neutral spine (no arching or rounding the low back) throughout the entire exercise. If you're using a regular barbell, you'll follow these same steps but hold the bar directly in front of you, hands about shoulder-width apart.

Single-Arm Dumbbell Row

How to: Start in a split stance (one foot in front of the other), back flat, and torso leaning slightly forward. Hold a dumbbell in the opposite hand of the front foot. Your other hand should be on a box or bench to support your weight.

a) With the dumbbell hanging directly under your shoulder, pull it up toward your hip.

b) Lower it back to the starting position and repeat.

c) Finish all reps on one side before switching to the other.

Form focus: It's common to want to shrug your shoulders up toward your ears during this move. But instead, roll your shoulders down your back; you'll want to hit the opposite position of hunching over a computer.

Back Squat

How to: With a barbell in the racked position, stand under it so the barbell is behind your head and resting on your traps (the muscle in your upper back that runs from your neck to just below your shoulder blade). Grasp the bar with both hands just outside shoulder-width.

a) Unrack the bar and carefully take one step back with each foot. Feet should be hip-width apart or just slightly wider, toes pointing slightly outward.

b) Take a big breath into your belly, tighten your abs, and drive your elbows toward the floor. As you hinge at the hips and bend your knees, sit straight down into a squat. Go as low as you can without your back rounding. Ideally, you want your hip crease lower than the top of your knee.

c) Stand straight back up, without locking your knees at the top.

d) Repeat.

Form focus: The goal is to sit your body straight down between your ankles while keeping your torso upright. Keep your weight in your heels and look forward throughout the entire exercise.

Overhead Press

How to: Hold a barbell at your collar bones, hands just outside shoulder width, and feet directly under hips.

a) Engaging your abs, press the bar straight up, passing it close to your face.

b) Once the bar passes your forehead, press it back slightly so it ends up over the base of your neck at the top of the movement.

c) Slowly and with control, bring the bar back down to just above your collar bone.

d) Repeat.

Form focus: Too many people finish with the bar forward, over the bridge of the nose. This leads to an unstable overhead position, so aim to push it up and just slightly back.

Bench Press

How to: Lie on your back on a bench with feet planted firmly on the floor. Your eyes should be directly under the bar.

a) Grab the bar, with hands just outside shoulder width. Then unrack it and hold it over your chest.

b) Lower the bar to your chest or just above it if you don't have the full range of motion.

c) Drive the bar straight up again.

d) Repeat before re-racking.

Form focus: While a slight arch in your lower back is OK, try to keep your back against the bench as much as you can through this move. Also, pull your elbows in toward your ribcage as you lower the bar to keep them from flaring out to the sides.

Chin-Ups

How to: Start with your hands on a stable bar, about shoulder-width apart, palms facing you and elbows straight.

a) With abs engaged, toes pointed, and legs straight and slightly in front of your torso, drive your elbows down toward the floor and pull your chest up to the bar.

b) Slowly lower yourself back down and repeat.

Form focus: There's no shame in needing assistance for this one. Grab a resistance band and loop it around your feet to help you pull yourself up.

Now, last but not least:

Supplements

Dietary supplement recommendations can be found everywhere—on commercials, through social media influencers, and from your neighbors, friends, and family. Amid the noise, it can be hard to know which supplement, if any, is right for you. Though many supplements are certainly beneficial to your health, evidence varies widely, and it's important to know which can benefit your health and which may be harmful.

5 Things You Need to Know About Dietary Supplements

1. Supplements come in many forms.
Whether in pill, powder, or liquid form, the goal of dietary supplements is often the same: to supplement your diet to get enough nutrients and enhance health.

They contain at least one dietary ingredient, such as vitamins, minerals, herbs, botanicals, amino acids, or enzymes. Some of the most popular supplements come in a multivitamin (which can help you avoid taking a dozen pills each day), but they can also be purchased as a standalone supplement. The simplest common denominator? They're labeled as dietary supplements. Some common dietary supplements include:

Calcium
Fish oil

Echinacea

Ginseng

Garlic

Vitamin D

St. John's wort

Green tea

2. *Some supplements are effective, while others are not.*
There's a reason supplements are so popular: sometimes, they work. Common supplements that may benefit your health include:

Vitamin B12, which can help keep nerve and blood cells healthy, make DNA, and prevent anemia.

Folic acid, which can reduce birth defects when taken by pregnant women.

Vitamin D, which can strengthen bones.

Calcium, which can promote bone health.

Vitamins C and E, which can prevent cell damage.

Fish oil, which can support heart health.

Vitamin A, which can slow down vision loss from age-related macular degeneration.

Zinc, which can promote skin health and slow down vision loss from age-related macular degeneration.

Melatonin, which can help counteract jet lag.

Despite the amount of research that's been done on supplements (since 1999, the National Institutes of

Health has spent more than $2.4 billion studying vitamins and minerals), scientific evidence isn't completely clear.

Keep in mind: most studies suggest that multivitamins won't make you live longer, slow cognitive decline, or lower your chances of diseases such as heart disease, cancer, or diabetes. In fact, it's illegal for companies to make claims that supplements will treat, diagnose, prevent, or cure diseases. Also, the products you buy in stores or online may be different from those used in studies, so studies may be misleading.

3. Supplements aren't always safe.

In most cases, multivitamins aren't likely to pose any health risks. Still, it's important to be cautious when you put anything in your body.

Supplements may interact with other medications you're taking or pose risks if you have certain medical conditions such as liver disease, or if you are going to have surgery. Some supplements also haven't been tested in pregnant women, nursing mothers, or children, and you may need to take extra precautions. Also, federal regulations for dietary supplements are less strict than prescription drugs. Some supplements may contain ingredients not listed on the label, and these ingredients can be unsafe.

Certain products are marketed as dietary supplements and actually contain prescription drugs within them, drugs that are not allowed in dietary supplements.

4. *Some supplements that may pose risks include:*

Vitamin K, which can reduce the effectiveness of blood thinners.

Ginkgo, which can increase blood thinning.

St. John's wort, which can make some drugs, such as antidepressants and birth control, less effective.

Herbal supplements comfrey and kava, which can damage your liver.

Beta-carotene and vitamin A, which can increase the risk of lung cancer in smokers.

5. *Speak with your healthcare provider before taking any supplements.*

The most important thing to remember is to be smart when choosing a supplement.

Your first step should be discussing your options with your healthcare provider since a supplement's effectiveness and safety may depend on your individual situation and health.

On top of that, keep these simple tips in mind as you choose a supplement:

Take supplements as directed according to the label and your healthcare provider's instructions.

Read the label, including ingredients, drug interactions, and percent daily value (percent DV).

Be wary of extreme claims, such as "completely safe" or "works better than [insert prescription drug]."

Remember that the term "natural" doesn't necessarily equal "safe." Keep supplements stored properly and away from children.

✪ ✪ ✪

Circling back to the mental toughness. I get up at 3:30 in the morning, I do a four-hour radio show, then I go to post-show meetings. By the time I get home, I'm exhausted. I then walk thirteen New York city blocks to get to the gym. I could take the train, or I could take a cab, but I don't. I walk. I go next door to Starbucks to get myself a double espresso just to wake up, and I drink that thing in about thirty seconds. But I have to tell you, on the walk to the gym, if it's a cold day, a blustery day, or even one hundred degrees and humid, three or four times in that thirteen-block walk, I'll consider turning around and going home. At least three or four times. But I never do. Two hours later, when I'm finished with my workout, I feel like a million bucks.

My wife, for example, gets up at 4:30 in the morning and runs because she's a marathon runner. She's finished thirty-one of them, including six New York City Marathons. She makes the time to run at that hour because she has to be at work early in the morning.

I'm the opposite. Although I also work very early in the morning, I can't do anything before I head to the station because my gym isn't even open. I have to do it after the show, which makes it even more difficult, but believe me when I tell you, I get it done.

People say to me all the time, "Oh, you look great."

I say, "Well, yeah, I go to the gym five or six days a week. What do you do?"

I'll often get a response like, "I went to the gym twice last week, and I took a SoulCycle class." That's fine if you're thin, but if you're not and want to lose a significant amount of weight, or want to get big and put on muscle, you need to put in the work.

It's like anything else in life: if you want to become a good basketball player, you've got to practice your jump shot; if you want to become a good baseball player, you have to hit in the batting cages and field ground balls; and if you want to be a great golfer, you better be at the range if you're not playing eighteen.

Getting in shape is no different. You've got to be there at the gym, you have to be dedicated, and you have to do it consistently all week long. So, when you start missing days and making excuses, don't bitch and complain when somebody says, "Hey, Sid looks great, and you look like Rosie O'Donnell chowing down on Olive Garden's never-ending pasta bowl."

SID-IZEN SUGGESTION

If you're serious about wanting to work out, get fit, and get in shape and don't know what to do or where to start, I would advise you to get a trainer. Eventually, with the trainer, if that person is good, after a couple of months you're going to start to realize you know what to do yourself. At that point you won't need a trainer.

Now, I know people who have a lot of money, tons and tons of money, and they've had trainers their entire lives. Every time they work out, it's with a trainer. That's a great luxury if you can swing it. Truth is, it's always fun to work out with somebody else, and you'll get the extra motivation of having a professional telling you, "Do that set! Do this set!" which always helps get results faster. But it takes a lot of money.

So, if you don't have a lot of money to burn and you're a nine-to-five working guy or gal? When you first start at a gym, use a trainer. Write everything down. Then start by yourself.

Bottom line is, we're all aging. Be smart and listen to your body. Obviously, as we get older, our bodies change. Maybe your joints aren't the same as they used to be, so you have to be a little less aggressive. That's fine. Go at your own pace.

I know guys who bench press 275 pounds, and when they feel something start to hurt, they dial it down. When your body starts to tell you it ain't working, then it ain't working.

I remember one time I hurt my shoulder really bad. I was getting intramuscular shots; I was getting epidurals; I was a complete mess. I couldn't even sit straight. In the studio with Bernie, I'd have to constantly be walking around the room because my shoulder and arm were killing me. I ended up doing muscular and nerve damage in my neck and shoulders.

Right before I injured myself, I was lifting a lot of weight, and a guy at the gym walked over to me and said, "Let me ask you a question. How old are you?" At the time I was fifty-one.

He said, "How long you want to play this game?"

I said, "Game? What game?"

He shot back, "This game, this weightlifting game. How long do you plan on playing?"

I said, "Well, hopefully forever."

He said, "Well, doing what you're doing right now? It ain't gonna happen."

At this point, I was a tad surprised, confused, and a little bit pissed off. "What do you mean?!"

He said, "You can't lift that type of weight. You're going to get hurt."

No less than two weeks later, I ended up with the worst sports injury in my life. The guy was right. I learned my lesson: don't be such a tough guy, because the idea is to keep playing the game. That's the key.

Be responsible and, for God's sake, at least once in a while put down the remote and get off your tuchus. There's no time for excuses. It's later than you think.

CHAPTER FOUR

SID'S REALITY

Here's the reality of the situation, folks: my name is Sid Rosenberg, and I'm a reality TV addict.

It all began on an innocent night of endless channel surfing until I landed on Bravo…then I saw it—I saw Teresa Giudice, a cast member of *The Real Housewives of New Jersey*, sitting at a table in a restaurant with a bunch of other yapping broads, and she starts to get crazy. I mean DEFCON 1, water boiling over the pot, batshit crazy. She picks up a table and throws it. Everything goes flying, broads start screaming, chaos ensues, and I'm thinking, What the hell is this? I don't know, but whatever it is, I have to watch! From that moment on, I was hooked.

I'm not alone. Hundreds of millions of people all around the world are addicted to reality TV, and it turns out there are psychological reasons for this occurrence. Many studies have been performed to try to pinpoint the exact reason many of us are so fascinated by reality television. The misconception that arose before studies were conducted was that reality television fans were less intelligent than people who hate reality TV. Not true.

As if you need to be a doctor of philosophy with a degree from Harvard to sit through and comprehend an entire half-hour episode of *Friends*. You don't. Anyone can do it. You just need a lot of patience and booze. Fortunately, for people like myself who enjoy their weekly dose of this genre, intelligence has not been linked as a determining factor in who does or does not enjoy *Keeping Up with the Kardashians*.

So, here are some of the top reasons why reality TV is so addictive. Let's get into it:

Competitive Nature

It has been found that people who have a competitive nature are more likely to watch reality televisions shows in a similar way that people enjoy watching sports. Many shows have the premise of competing for a prize (*The Bachelor, So You Think You Can Dance, American Idol, Project Runway, Survivor, The Voice, America's Next Top Model, Top Chef,* and so on).

Constant Exposure

Whether we are aware of it or not, the media influences us every single day. It may be through social media, in the checkout line via magazines, or commercials. We are constantly being exposed to so-called celebrities and influencers. Unfortunately, the more we see Kim Kardashian in the media, the more we subconsciously become invested and interested in her life. This is one of the main reasons why reality TV is so addictive, and for me, one of the drawbacks.

Social Experimentation/Challenging Norms

What happens if you have a group of Guido strangers living together in a house on the Jersey Shore for the summer? What about making twenty women compete for the affection of one man? How do people act when you make a person go on three dates and choose one winner?

Many premises of reality television shows revolve around social experimentation. On many shows you can see a fictional depiction of what might go on with manipulation of contestants by producers. Taking unlikely scenarios and making people live in them is a much less severe form of dystopian reality that intrigues many people.

Un/Candid Authenticity

Producers may manipulate what we actually see, but our perceived reality is that we are watching people in an unfiltered, authentic way. When cameras are following people around 24/7, we can relate to certain scenarios that may mimic our own lives.

Source of Entertainment

There's a thing called the social comparison theory. Basically, the theory explains the way people determine their self-confidence/worth is by comparing themselves to others (this is why social media can have such a negative effect on people) and determining whether or not they are better or worse off.

When it comes to reality television, it can make people feel better about themselves on many occasions. For example, watching fifty-year-old broads on (insert any *Housewives* series here) get shit-faced drunk and make complete fools of themselves can make you feel infinitely better about your own social faux pas. This is a huge reason why reality TV is so addictive.

Envy

In some cases, it can have the opposite effect. Many people are watching because they are envious. If you don't live a life of privilege, and you are watching people who appear to have lots of money to spend on their appearance and clothing, you can fantasize about a life of luxury and fame.

Comparing your own possessions, wealth, and social life to others in this way can have a negative effect. Envy can make people more jealous and generally pissed off.

Living Vicariously

People read, watch movies, and watch television shows that are fiction in order to experience something they may never experience. When you add an element of reality to television shows, it takes real-life situations and lets people watch them unfold from the comfort of their own couches.

We can watch ridiculous forms of debauchery/sexual promiscuity, rash drama, foul-mouthed drunks, people get engaged in three months, and the like without doing any of it in our own lives, and, boy, it feels good.

It's Mindless

At the end of a long day at the office or in classes when your brain is fried, the last thing you want to do is something strenuous. When you watch reality television, it is not imperative that you pay attention to every single detail in order to follow a basic plotline, which makes it perfect for recharging the mental batteries.

Drama

Whenever I hear someone say they don't want drama in their lives and go to any lengths to avoid it, I automatically think, Bullshit! Drama is exciting. It makes us feel busy, responsible, and involved. It also helps us feel ourselves in a concrete and emotional way. Our heart is pumping, we're impassioned, and a sense of self-righteousness may overtake us. We feel like we're responding in a powerful way. Face it, there's a drama queen in all of us.

Small Talk

Lastly, since many of us do watch reality television shows, it is an easy way to connect to people and make small talk. If you want something to talk about with that bitch Linda in accounting in the break room when you're pouring your second cup of coffee at 10 a.m. on a Tuesday, then discussing your favorite reality TV shows is a good way to find common ground.

✪ ✪ ✪

Except for *The Sopranos* and *Sex and the City* (I love both) my drift away from mainstream sitcoms and dramas has been in the making for quite a while. I never really got into *Seinfeld*, never got into *Friends*, or any of those shows. I never fell in love with the sitcoms of the eighties and nineties.

Even in the last ten years, I never thought successful mainstream hits like *Modern Family* were all that good. So, I started to like what I saw on network TV less and less, and this was right before Netflix became big and Amazon Prime, Google, and Apple.

Today you've got nine million different channels to choose from, and with On Demand you can now watch whatever you want whenever you want. Because of these new streaming outlets, it seems like there's a new reality show out every night of the week.

But where did this phenomenon come from? What were its origins? Some say the first reality show was *Survivor*, others say *The Real World*. I don't think it was either of them. I think to find the answer we have to dig a little deeper into history to answer the questions: What is reality television and where did it come from? Let's get into it:

What Is Reality TV?

What the hell is it? Reality TV is the projection of people's lives in real or fabricated situations and can range from documentary-style informative shows, entertainment shows based on the lives of reality TV actors, game shows, contests, talent auditions, adventure programs, housing shows, philanthropy, love and dating shows, shows that outline the inner workings of a particular industry, and so much more. Thus, it can be difficult to outline what exactly reality TV is and what reality television isn't.

Shows like *Big Brother* that show everyday people in a prolonged living environment ultimately competing for a contest would definitely be considered reality TV. The "actors" are everyday people often interested in TV careers, their conversations are not scripted, and the reactions of the actors are completely genuine as they are documented in real time.

However, shows like the late Steve Irwin's *The Crocodile Hunter*, which are largely informational and follow a scripted outline, could be considered reality TV, and while shows like this do in fact involve the reality of Steve Irwin (for this particular example) doing things in his life, in real time, and in situations that are real for him, the reality of the program is far removed as reality for everyday people. While Steve Irwin's show would probably not be considered traditional reality TV, you could make a strong argument that while onscreen Steve Irwin is doing things he might do during his normal job, even if the show is scripted to portray a particular theme for that week.

For example, Steve Irwin's show involved him as the main character season after season. This is true for several reality TV programs that highlight a professional within a particular industry. *Big Brother*, however, constantly changes its actors in order to keep audience interest and to remain true to the show's contest-style format. Thus, a reality program can be portrayed and involve almost a million different subjects, "actors," and themes depending on the program.

Therefore, in answering what is reality TV, the answer can be any form of television that touches on the reality of people's lives. While many fictional shows do in fact touch on real issues or portray real stories, reality TV is generally reserved for nonprofessional actors and stays focused on the lives of the actors as their lives are currently happening.

The History of Reality TV

Even though the term "reality television" is largely used to identify shows that have emerged since the year 2000, the history of reality TV goes back much farther. This is in large part due to the broadness of the term "reality television" and the many ways in which aspects of reality and daily life are integrated into what people like to watch on television. Since its conception, television has been portraying the lives of people through dating shows, contests, and pranks, giving reality television a much broader history than most people might think when considering modern reality television and its boom in popularity in recent years.

In looking back through history, it's interesting to see where the foundation for this genre really began. One of history's most famous reality TV shows emerged in the late forties, when Allen Funt brought *Candid Camera* into the lives of millions of people. This show, which highlighted funny pranks and humorous situations being pulled on the unknown masses, was an instant hit and remained on the air for years. Today, versions of prank-style reality programming still exist in *America's Funniest Home Videos*, MTV's *Punk'd*, *Jackass*, and other prank-style variety shows. Humor at the hand of an unknown bystander has its roots alongside the root of television itself in a reality television format that has proven to consistently deliver for audiences and is one that continues to be loved, used, and watched by many.

Aside from jokes and hijinks, contest-style reality TV shows have proven to be a crowd favorite throughout the history of television. Shows such as the *Miss America Pageant*, which first aired in the early 1950s, have continued to remain one of the largest themes in reality TV for decades. Contest-based reality TV has been a tried-and-true format for entertainment throughout the years and continues to be. *American Idol* is one such contest-style reality show that has not only become one of the most popular reality-based television shows in history but consistently pulls in some of the highest ratings in television among both reality-based and fictional television programs. These competition-style reality programs, which began in the fifties, have been a successful model for modern reality TV as we see it today.

In the seventies, shows that outlined a more somber view of people's lives began to gain popularity with programs like PBS's *An American Family*, which showed a traditional American family going through the stressors of a divorce. This format is more reminiscent of the reality television that we see today, which tries to go behind the scenes of a situation that is popular or of great interest to audiences.

Within this same time period, *The Dating Game*, *The Newlywed Game*, and other relationship-style reality programming was introduced, proving just how interesting audiences found the lives, love lives, and dating struggles of their peers.

These early formats, or the fundamentals behind these formats rather, gained a lot of ground during the seventies and eighties bringing shows like MTV's *The Real World* and *COPS*, two shows that are considered pioneers in the history of reality television, to the forefront. These two shows, although dramatically different in tone and style, represent two arenas of reality television that have since become incredibly popular. In a way very voyeuristic, MTV's *The Real World* began to a large degree the modern world's fascination with watching the lives of everyday people interacting with one another and fueled this interest in modern reality television.

While in recent years the number of reality television programs has increased incredibly compared to what was being watched in years past, many of the formats are the same. From the time television was born, people were fascinated with seeing everyday people fight, claw, cry, laugh, love, struggle, work, and find their way, all to the delight of the viewer. So, undoubtedly, the history of reality TV has really paved the way for many of today's most popular television shows.

Which leads me back my go-to reality show: *The Real Housewives of New Jersey*. After Teresa's table flipping, I started watching every variation of the series: New York, Orange County, Atlanta, Beverly Hills, Salt Lake City, all of them.

Listen, I understand none of these women are going to find a cure for cancer. I got it. We probably all know women like these in our real lives. Women with similar personalities, living in New York or New Jersey surrounded by material stuff like the big houses, the fancy cars, and the goombah boyfriends. Because of that familiar relatability combined with ridiculously silly plot lines, it makes these shows an easy watch...

...at least they used to be an easy watch. Now, like most things, they've been bitten by the woke bug, for example, Eboni K. Williams (the newest cast member of *Real Housewives of New York*), whom I knew from her days at WABC. She used to work with Curtis Sliwa, and she became pretty friendly with my wife Danielle and me. She was also co-hosting a daily show on Fox News with Eric Bolling and Kat Timpf called *The Fox News Specialists*. She kind of disappeared for a while and recently reemerged on the show, where she is just unbearable. She's trying to mix in with the other ladies who are in their fifties and sixties, ladies who are set in their ways and aren't very bright, to be honest, and attempt to make them aware of Black history and Black this and Black that; it is utterly ridiculous.

I mean, in the first episode she's wearing a hoodie with an image of the Central Park Five, which is bullshit. She was not like that when she worked my radio station. She was not like that when she worked at Fox News. I'm not sure if that's what the producers or Andy Cohen want her to do on the show, but if it's a character, it's unbearable; if it's her, she's changed an awful lot in the last couple of years, so I can't watch New York anymore. I can't do it. They're clearly taking a cue from liberal media's obsession with wokeness, and viewers are turning their TVs off! With extremely low ratings, Bravo's choice to chastise white people can be considered an epic failure. Despite what liberals say, not everything needs to be about race, and that includes catfighting women on the Upper East Side.

Eboni K. Williams was brought on to the cast, not as an old friend who has an already forged connection with the ladies, but as a newbie playing in-house woke police with no prior connections that would justify her being among this tight-knit group of ladies. "I'm a little bit of a preacher and I wear that as a badge of honor. And I'm a little bit of a teacher too," Eboni said in regard to her persona on the show.

In one episode, Eboni decides to host a party in Harlem and then give a lesson on Black people to the rest of the cast. When did this become *The Real Housewives of Alternate History*? Bring back Dorinda. Bring back Tinsley. Let them loose in the Hamptons with a camera crew, a case of Ramona Pinot, and their own impulses. We'll learn a lot more and laugh a lot more too.

Bravo has been doing a great job of isolating their audience. They built an entire brand off of what would be considered "white privilege," and now they are playing the race card. Can't have it both ways. These shows have always been about rich people's shenanigans, vapid drama, and lots of chardonnay. This is not and has never been MSNBC with lip filler!

Even the actor Michael Rapaport feels the same way, and he can be impossible, but he agrees with me that those shows are not meant to be political. New Jersey is not like that, thank God; they remain true to what they do. But shows like *New York* and *Beverly Hills* have become very disappointing. Very.

Is it possible this franchise has jumped the shark? Sure, it is. How many times can somebody throw over a table? How many times can somebody get divorced? What other story lines can there possibly be? At the end of the day, these are still real people with kids, grandkids, moms, and dads, so you can't make it too crazy. You can't have one housewife sleeping with the husband of another housewife; you can't do it.

✪ ✪ ✪

Now, sure "reality stars" are on TV, many of them are household names, but can you classify them in the same league as other celebrities like famous movie or TV stars and top-tier athletes? This is a question I'll often get asked. Let me tell you, I have been to events with reality people where their fans are crying in their presence. I mean really crying, yelling, screaming. I'm talking thousands of people with the same reaction, if not even crazier than they'd be in front of their favorite movie or TV acting celeb.

Why is this? It's because at the end of the day these "actors" and "actresses" on reality shows are relatable to people like you and me, and traditionally "famous" actors like Robert De Niro and Julia Roberts simply aren't. George Clooney and Meryl Streep are making $20 million a movie living in a guarded mansion, and you're some schlub who lives in Brooklyn, or Paterson, New Jersey; how can you possibly relate to them? You can't.

When you see some of these girls on *Real Housewives*, they're just more relatable. In New Jersey, when they go to a diner or restaurant, they're actually there. The big-time actors, you hardly ever see them in public, and if you do see them in a restaurant, they're most likely in a private room, a long way away from where you and I are having our clams casino appetizer.

So, for the fans of these reality shows, their reaction is even crazier because the people on these shows are relatable. You can touch them, you can feel them, and they're much, much, much nicer to their fans—most of them, not all of them—than the big Hollywood stars.

What do traditionally famous celebs think of "reality stars"? Well, they think they're shit. Beneath them. Common gentry that lucked into the celebrity club with an unearned backstage pass. For example, take this encounter from a few years ago between Martha Stewart and Luann de Lesseps, as reported by the *NY Post*:

> The two women were dinner guests of Qatari Ambassador to the US, Mohammed Jaham Al Kuwari, who was having a lovely chat with de Lesseps

and inviting her to visit his country. "He said he knew that she was on a TV show and that he would love to be on it, and Stewart leaned in and whispered, 'You don't want to do that. It's lowbrow, very B-list.' The countess—battle-hardened from her years on "The Real Housewives of New York City"—said loudly, "Martha, I can hear you." The doyenne of domesticity tried to backtrack, saying she was only kidding, but de Lesseps said, "Should I tell him about your shady past?"—a reference to Stewart's prison stint for dissembling to the feds in an insider-trading probe.

How ridiculous is this? Martha Stewart makes hundreds of millions of dollars. These girls on *Housewives* (with the exemption of one or two) don't make that. A couple Housewives make seven-figure salaries, but most of the girls don't get near it. In fact, most Housewives are working six or seven days a week, running all over town, going to every event to supplement their income because they do live nicely, and they are, quote, unquote "stars on TV," but the overwhelming majority make a couple hundred thousand.

So, for anybody like Martha Stewart who is worth hundreds of millions to be obsessed with Luann or any other Housewife is really petty. Really. Petty.

✪ ✪ ✪

I'm not just a one-trick pony when it comes to my reality TV viewing habits. Meaning, I'm not just a *Housewives* guy. I watch most of the shows on Bravo. I like *Southern Charm*, which takes place in Charleston, South Carolina. I like the *Shahs of Sunset*, about the Iranian folks who live in Los Angeles. I also like all those real estate shows. The ones in New York and Los Angeles with Josh Altman, Josh Flagg, and Fredrik Eklund, a former New York guy now on the LA show.

Honestly most of the time I hate-watch it because I could never buy a $40 million dollar house. Few people can. So, based on that fact, I don't know why anybody is even watching it.

Other than that, it's interesting to see the negotiations, and some of the guys like Flagg and Altman can be very entertaining but also very douchey. Very. Douchey. Which keeps me watching.

On the other hand, you couldn't pay me to watch shows like *Dr. Pimple Popper*. However, I do still watch *Jersey Shore*, all the time, even though they're older and uglier. But it's MTV, E!, and Bravo, that get my attention, all three of those networks.

Now are shows like *Shark Tank* considered a reality show or game show? For me, it's a game show. I've watched it a couple of times, but I generally don't like a few of the "Sharks" on the show. First of all, I can't stand Mark Cuban; he thinks he's king of the world, and the bald guy Kevin O'Leary is a condescending prick. I always felt badly for the people up there begging for money. For me, it seems kind of humiliating. I know sometimes they'll get a deal, which will help start their careers and give them the possibility to be a success if they make it, but most of the time I'm watching, I'm humiliated for the contestants.

What about *The Apprentice*? I liked it. You had ten or twelve people who had to do a task, and eventually somebody won. Sometimes they had to do things they didn't like to do, but at least they weren't begging Donald Trump for a 9 percent investment in organic socks. They'd go into the boardroom, and he'd say, "You're fired! Get the hell out." So, I like that dynamic and format much more than what *Shark Tank* presents to the viewer.

Now, have I ever been approached to do a reality show, you ask? Well, yes, I have. Next season, I'll be on an episode of *Real Housewives of New Jersey* appearing in a celebrity softball game in Brooklyn as manager of one of the teams.

The only other time I was on what could be considered "reality TV" was when I hosted *Wack Pack Bowling* on Howard TV in 2008, which was a blast.

We filmed in a building in Harlem. I got off the elevator on the fourth floor, the door opens, and sitting on a couch is none other than *Wack Pack* hall-of-famers Beetlejuice,

Elephant Boy, and Ronnie the limo driver. There was a table set up with bagels and not orange juice, but vodka at 7:45 in the morning. I knew we were in for a great day, and we were. We taped like twelve shows, and I was there until about five or six at night, and it was an absolute blast.

I'm often asked if my better half, Danielle, would be on a reality show like the *Housewives*? She definitely has what it takes. She's unflappable and a tough, brilliant attorney. There's not a Housewife around that's going to intimidate Danielle. Ever.

So, could she, do it? Absolutely. Would she, do it? I don't know. I'd do it in a heartbeat. I've tried to get on *Watch What Happens Live with Andy Cohen*, which is a late-night show on Bravo, and they've always got two people on the show at once. Usually, it's one or two of the Housewives or anyone from one of the Bravo shows, but sometimes Michael Rapaport is there, or Jerry O'Connell is there, and I'm like hey, I'm a huge Bravo fan, I'm better looking than all those guys, I'm in great shape, and I host a very popular top-rated morning show in New York. Put me in the clubhouse! I can kibitz hot topics with the best of them. Don't believe me? Just watch my appearance on *The Wendy Williams Show* (Wendy is a big fan and listens to Bernie and me every morning).

Recently Andy Cohen was on my radio show, and he said, "Sid we're going to get it done." Predictably, nothing has happened since.

SID-IZEN SUGGESTION

Listen, I still find this reality TV bullshit entertaining. I really do. Some of these women I know personally are really great ladies, and I'll still watch. I won't watch it when it gets political. I'll shut that off right away.

But I still watch enough of the *Housewives* shows and the other Bravo shows to say, I'm a big fan, and I think people should give it a shot. At least it's less depressing than (enter any MSNBC or CNN news show here).

Even with Donald Trump, who as you know, I think was a great president, the news was depressing. Now it's just overboard with this imbecile Joe Biden.

So, once in a while if you want to watch a silly show for an hour about a bunch of good looking fifty-year-old ladies and who they're shtupping and what they're driving and all that type of nonsense, then please switch it on and forget about all the other serious bullshit we have to deal with on a day-to-day basis.

CHAPTER FIVE

THE GOAT

I n any sport, "GOAT" stands for "Greatest of All Time." Thomas Edward Patrick Brady can only be described in one acronym: GOAT. The Greatest of All Time. Being the 199th pick of the 2000 NFL Draft, Brady has always had to fight against the odds.

That is what makes his story that much better than the next. It wasn't expected of him. He wasn't expected to be anything more than a career backup quarterback.

I've been in arguments over the years with "know-it-all" blowhards like Dan Le Batard, who would preach from the pulpit of Peyton, emphatically claiming that Manning was better than Brady. I disagreed. Le Batard was wrong. I was right. (As I always was in debates with Le Batard, regardless of topic.)

Why is Tom Brady the GOAT?

Let's get into it:

The Seven Lombardi Trophies

Seven rings. At the end of the day, the rings are all that matter. QB ratings, passing yards, and TDs aren't worth a lick of salt if you aren't winning. If you think anything but Super Bowls matter, ask Jerry Jones. Jones wants another Super Bowl win for his beloved Dallas Cowboys more than anything.

Suppose you sat down and talked to any of the elite quarterbacks who never won a Super Bowl. What would they wish for above all else? That's precisely my point. Dan Marino smashed passing records during a career with the Miami Dolphins. Still, he could never lead his team to a Lombardi Trophy. While there's no disputing Marino was an excellent passer, he's not even in the conversation of the best quarterbacks of all time. He was at one point, then all of Brady's contemporaries came along.

No QB Has Appeared in as Many Super Bowls

Tom Brady gets his team to the Super Bowl. Brady has appeared in ten Super Bowls total throughout his career. The next closest quarterback is John Elway with five. There's no disputing that hitting double digits in Super Bowl appearances is something truly remarkable. Brady has appeared in more Super Bowls than John Elway and Joe Montana combined. And he has won more Super Bowls than Roger Staubach, Peyton Manning, and Brett Favre combined. Of course, the list grows much larger if we add quarterbacks who were elite but never won the big game.

He Won Against the All-Time Greats

It's not as if Brady was playing against weak competition. Many of the all-time passing leaders went head-to-head with Brady and fell short. Brady faced several of the best, but his rivalry with Peyton Manning stood out the most. Brady and Manning faced off fifteen times in the NFL playoffs. Even Manning's two Super Bowls and five MVPs seem weak in comparison to what Brady has accomplished. Manning is easily a first-ballot Hall of Fame quarterback. Yet, Brady has surpassed the legend in nearly every way imaginable—much like he has every other player to ever stand under center.

The Numbers Don't Lie

Tom Brady has put himself near the top in every metric that makes an NFL quarterback elite. He's in the top five all time in passing yards and touchdown passes. Brady has more play-off wins than anyone and has won twelve divisional titles, more than any of the other greats. Brady isn't just the best to ever do it; he's closed the door on the conversation. Many people hated on Brady for years, but, like Le Batard, they were all wrong. Brady is fantastic, and they probably wish they had spent more time appreciating the greatness as it was happening.

He's at His Best in the Playoffs

The NFL playoffs are the bar by which all NFL quarterbacks are measured. You cannot deny or argue the overwhelming success of Brady in the playoffs. He rises to the occasion where so many others have merely folded under the pressure.

Joe Montana has long been considered the best of all time with his four Super Bowl rings. Terry Bradshaw is another of the greats and one of only three QBs to have four rings. Tom Brady is now sitting with seven. So, if Super Bowl wins are the measure of greatness, it's not even a discussion about who the GOAT is anymore. Brady has not only continued to be a tremendous contender at the top of the NFL, but he's also shown sustained success for going on twenty years.

All Expectations Have Been Vastly Exceeded

To say that Brady has exceeded every expectation would be an understatement. Even if Brady had been selected first overall, anybody would clearly understand what a once-in-a-lifetime talent Brady is. The Pats took Brady 199th overall. If I listed the 198 players that were taken ahead of him, you'd probably recognize fewer than five. Brian Urlacher, the former Chicago Bears linebacker, is the most notable selection outside of Brady. He's a player who very well could have gone undrafted but turned out to be the best. Even the talking heads at Disney must be jealous of that story line!

Nobody Has Been as Clutch

Tom Brady, in a word, is "clutch." There's not a person on the planet you'd rather have the ball than Tom Brady when the game is on the line. In the first Super Bowl he played in, Brady marched down the field in a tied game with under two minutes on the clock and got the Patriots within field goal range. From that moment on, Brady has never let his teammates down. I believe it's this same determination that carried the Buccaneers into the Super Bowl last season. Brady clearly does not falter in the face of overwhelming pressure, and by this point, how much stress can he truly feel moving forward? He's pretty much done it all.

He Has Defied Age

Seriously, the guy has hardly aged. It's clear that he's lost a little mobility, and the cannon is beginning to fade, but he's still the best even at forty-four. To put that in context, Patrick Mahomes, who faced Brady in Super Bowl LV, was only four years old when the Patriots drafted Brady in the 2000 NFL Draft. Brady hasn't taken shortcuts like discovering the fountain of youth. He's stayed relevant through hard work and discipline. Brady has a daily regimen that he sticks to 365 days a year. He doesn't gain twenty pounds in the off-season or rush back into shape before the team reports for training camp. Would it surprise anybody if he were around for another five years? Nope.

He's Made More Out of Less

Brady has won more Super Bowls than any quarterback in the history of the National Football League, and he's done it with less talent on paper than many. That's because Tom Brady makes everyone around him better. He's not making Wes Welker catch the ball. (If you recall, during the Patriots' 21–17 loss to the Giants in Super Bowl XLVI, after the game Gisele Bündchen was famously caught on camera saying, "My husband cannot f---ing throw the ball and catch the ball at the same time." That comment was directed at Welker for dropping an easy catch during the final minutes of the game.) However, Welker knows that he has to be where he's supposed to be, and if he is, the ball will be there immediately. There's no room for fractions or half effort in Brady's offense. This is a big reason why a fledgling slot receiver like Welker quickly became an All-Pro wide receiver. When Brady gets to throw to a tremendous wide receiver, you get the record season for TD receptions.

He's a Team-First Player

One of the impressive aspects to me is Brady's willingness to curb his ego and put the team first. He has demonstrated time and again that he will put the ability to win above his financial ambitions.

Brady served as the face of the franchise for two decades in Foxborough, and now for the last two seasons in Tampa, and he has never allowed arrogance to overshadow the team's accomplishments. He builds his teammates up when they win and places the responsibility squarely on his shoulders when they lose.

Brady has taken significantly less money off the field than he deserved in order to make sacrifices for the greater good. Brady is an excellent teammate both on and off the field.

✪   ✪   ✪

Brady's career accolades include seven Super Bowl wins, three MVP awards, fourteen Pro Bowls, three All-Pro teams, two Offensive Player of the Year awards, and the 2009 Comeback Player of the Year. Brady was also one of two players, with the other being a punter, named to the Pro Football Hall of Fame All-Decade Team twice. He was the First-Team quarterback on both the 2000's team and 2010's team.

Brady's career record is 230–69, a win percentage of 76.9. Added on to having the most wins in NFL history, he also has the best win percentage of quarterbacks who have started at least eighty-five games in the NFL. Brady has led the NFL in passing yards three times over his twenty-year career.

He has also led the league in passing touchdowns four times. Brady's 581 passing touchdowns are the most in NFL history as well. His 79,204 passing yards are just 1,154 yards behind the all-time passing yards leader, Drew Brees, who is expected to retire this off-season.

In his career, Tom Brady has made ten Super Bowl appearances. This means half of his seasons have ended in the Super Bowl. To put this into perspective, Brady has more Super Bowl appearances than thirty-one of thirty-two NFL teams. His seven Super Bowl wins are more than every NFL franchise.

Brady's playoff numbers are what truly set him above the rest. Brady has played in forty-five playoff games and has an outstanding 34–11 record. The next most playoff wins at the quarterback position is sixteen.

He has 12,449 passing yards in the playoffs, the most in NFL playoff history, and he is an astounding 5,110 yards above the second most (Peyton Manning).

The forty-four-year-old quarterback also has the most passing touchdowns in playoff history with eighty-three passing touchdowns, a large gap between the next most, Aaron Rodgers and Joe Montana (forty-five touchdowns).

Throughout Tom Brady's career, the narrative around him was that he was a system quarterback and had the best coach ever by his side, Bill Belichick. Going into the 2020–2021 NFL season, many predicted that Brady would have little to no success without his head coach.

When the season started slow for Tom Brady and the Tampa Bay Buccaneers, those who believed Brady was a system quarterback were loving it. The Bucs finished the 2019–2020 season with a 7–9 record and forty-one turnovers. With Brady at the helm in 2020–2021, they finished the season with an 11–5 record and seventeen turnovers, a drastic change.

Head Coach Bruce Arians gives the credit to Brady saying, "His leadership is off the charts…. He brought a winning mentality to a really talented football team that didn't know how to win…. [Brady's] preparation was unbelievable, but just how it rubs off on the rest of the football team."

Now, look, when he came to Tampa Bay, they put a lot of weapons around him. He has Evans, Fournette, Godwin, and they brought back Rob Gronkowski, as well as Antonio Brown at the recommendation of Brady, which we now know ended in disaster. So, now this guy has won in two different cities, at a very difficult position in a very difficult sport. There's only been four quarterbacks to go to Super Bowls with different teams: Brady with the Pats and Bucs, Peyton Manning with the Colts and Broncos, Kurt Warner with the Rams and Cardinals, and Craig Morton was with both Dallas and Denver. So, it's a very short list of guys.

The fact that this guy has won with two different teams, and now has a ring for every day of the week, and puts up big numbers with, again, the least complementary talent around him, makes Tom Brady the biggest winner and the greatest player of any sport. Ever.

He'll be forty-five by the time you're reading this. Obviously, he spends a lot of time working on his diet; he's got his own diet plan, which you can buy. You can eat the way Tom Brady does at home, of course, unfortunately, without Gisele.

As Brady continues to defy the trends of athletic performance, various questions percolate about his lifestyle habits. Is Tom Brady vegan? What does the TB12 diet consist of? What's Tom Brady's weight? How does one go about scoring his own Brazilian model wife? Okay, so maybe I can't help you with that last one, but for everything else, there's a logical explanation.

So, what's Tom Brady's diet and workout plan look like?

Let's get into it:

Tom Brady's Diet Plan

With his height of six foot four and estimated 225-pound weight, Tom Brady retains a relatively lean physique. Yet his body was famously awkward and lanky when he was first drafted to play in the NFL.

Over the years, he's fine-tuned his figure with considerable success. Indeed, many feel that he's never looked better than he does now. A dedicated training program is naturally responsible, but so, too, is a fairly meticulous diet plan.

Is Tom Brady vegan? The answer is no, though the TB12 diet may still surprise you. It consists primarily of whole foods and retains a thoroughly disciplined edge. When practiced, it can reportedly increase energy levels, reduce inflammation, ward off injuries, and bolster performance, among other things.

While some may say the proof is in the pudding (the pudding being Tom Brady's body, in this instance), others suggest that the TB12 diet isn't necessarily backed by hard science. Some argue that the diet is way too restrictive to maintain for extended periods of time. To which Brady himself might respond, "That's what cheat meals are for."

Critiques aside, Tom Brady's diet plan appears to work for him, and it could very well work for you too.

Here are some basic tenets of the program:

Consume organic, locally grown, seasonal, whole foods as much as possible. Try to avoid processed foods, added sugars, artificial sweeteners, trans fats, caffeine, monosodium glutamate (MSG), alcohol, iodized salt, dairy, nightshade vegetables, most oils, and most foods containing soy, GMOs, or gluten. Don't combine fruit with other foods. Don't combine high-protein foods (meat, fish, and the like) with carb-heavy foods (brown rice, bread, and the like). Drink half your body weight's worth of water per day, but avoid drinking water during or around meals. Try to time your meals and avoid eating within three hours of going to bed.

As you can see, Tom Brady's diet asks you to pay very careful attention to what you put into your body. It may even seem so restrictive that you're wondering what foods remain.

Now take a look at Brady's average *off-season meal plan* that looks something like this:

Wake up at 5:30 a.m. and drink a berry-and-banana smoothie, post-workout breakfast of eggs and avocado, lunch of salad with nuts and fish, snacks of hummus, guacamole, or mixed nuts throughout the day, dinner of roasted veggies and chicken.

Brady also said in a recent magazine interview that he's no stranger to the occasional cheat. "If I'm craving bacon, I have a piece. Same with pizza," he said. Nevertheless, if you want to lose weight Tom Brady-style, you should prepare to make some sacrifices.

Let's dig into it:

Tom Brady's Workout Routine

With help from personal trainer Alex Guerrero, Tom Brady remains in top physical form. During the off-season, he's been known to visit a private training facility in the Bahamas and put the TB12 workout to use. Generally speaking, he works out four to five days a week and even makes time for brain exercises.

In regard to both Guerrero's methods and the program itself, Brady said the following: "I absolutely know one hundred percent that it works, and the reality is I'm just a client who lives by the teachings." Here's a window into Tom Brady's workout routine during the off-season:

Wake up at 5:30 a.m., four-minute pre-workout massage (aka "deep force" treatment) from Guerrero, which targets twenty different muscle groups for approximately twenty seconds each.

Forty-minute resistance band workout; movement drills including squats, lunges, planks, and shoulder exercises; post-workout massage to increase blood flow, flush lactic acid, and expedite recovery time; fifteen minutes of online brain exercises by Posit Science BrainHQ, thereby enhancing visual precision and cognitive function.

As you may notice, Brady prefers resistance band training to regular weight training. This is in order to maintain a focus on speed, agility, and core stability. Unlike resistance bands, heavier weights can lead to tear-prone muscle fibers.

During the playing season, Tom Brady's workout takes on more intensity and complexity alike. With the goal of building strength, skill, recovery, and conditioning, Brady and Guerrero employ a nine-exercise program. Once again, resistance bands play a vital role. Here are some pointers from the TB12 workout:

Start exercises in a biomechanically neutral position (knees over feet, hips over knees, shoulders over hips, and so forth) so as to optimize form and activate the core. Use three different types of resistance bands during each overall workout: handle bands, long-looped bands, and short-looped bands. If a muscle group is exhausted or close to it, stop the exercise.

Combine strength-building and cardio by way of high-intensity resistance band workouts.

Emphasize ground force production.

Then we have a full-blown TB12 workout program, which looks something like this:

Warm-up: attach resistance bands over the shoulders so that they form an "X" on the chest, then run in place until you feel warmed up.

Exercise #1: banded standing row

Exercise #2: banded push-up

Exercise #3: banded core rotations

Exercise #4: dead lift

Exercise #5: bicep curl

Exercise #6: banded tricep extension

Exercise #7: deceleration lunges

Exercise #8: banded shoulder press

Exercise #9: X-band squat

✪ ✪ ✪

Can Brady play at age fifty?

I think he can. He takes his job seriously. You don't see Tom Brady out at three o'clock in the morning at nightclubs partying with Jay-Z and Beyoncé. Plus, his arm is still as accurate as ever, and he knows how to avoid getting hit. The guy just doesn't get sacked that often. So, unless he suffers some type of very debilitating injury, which at his age will be tough to come back from, there's no reason to believe this guy can't play until he's fifty, which would just be unbelievable.

SID-IZEN SUGGESTION

The 2021 season didn't end the way Brady and the Bucs planned, but love him or hate him, Tom Brady is the best to ever do it in the NFL and could be the best to ever do it in all of sports. And we're all relieved he's coming back after the entire football world waited with bated breath to see if this Brett Favre/Mike Francesa "retirement" spiel was the real thing. Thankfully for all of us, it wasn't, and TB will be back under center for the upcoming season. Now that Brady signed a ten-year deal with Fox for $375 Million, when he retires, he'll be in the booth with Kevin Burkhardt in a ratings competition with Joe Buck and Troy Aikman on ESPN, Jim Nance and Tony Romo on CBS, Mike Tirico and Chris Collinsworth on NBC, and now, Al Michaels on Amazon.

Tom was the GOAT on the field. Can he be the GOAT in the booth? The next John Madden? Only time will tell.

My recommendation is to sit back and enjoy the show. Always. Support. The GOAT…and Gisele.

CHAPTER SIX

WOKENESS
IN SPORTS

A wise man once said, "Everything woke turns to shit." First, let's get this out of the way: in my opinion the vast majority of sports fans—Black, brown, white, men, and women—don't care about the woke sports movement.

A recent poll shows that more than 30 percent of Americans say they have watched less sports over political and social justice messaging. The poll, conducted by Yahoo News/ YouGov, found 34.5 percent of respondents said they have watched less sports due to social justice campaigns. According to the poll, 11 percent of people said they have watched more sports as a result of the social justice messaging, and 56.3 percent said they have watched the same amount.

Looking at the different political party affiliations, 19 percent of Democrats said they have watched less sports in light of social justice messaging, while 13.7 percent said they have watched more. In comparison, 53 percent of Republicans said they have watched less sports due to social justice messaging, and just 8.6 percent said they have watched more. The poll also found that men were more likely to watch less sports as a result of social justice efforts, as 37.6 percent said so, compared to 28 percent of women.

In the several years since that moron Colin Kaepernick took a knee during the national anthem, sports have gone from a beautiful diversion to an ugly division. In baseball, the Cleveland Indians announced they will become the Cleveland Guardians. I don't know what these Guardians will guard other than fragile feelings of snowflakes who couldn't care less about the game but are offended by a name. In football, the once proud franchise of the Washington Redskins was publicly forced to change their name to the Commanders to appease the woke masses. In basketball, NBA players kneel for the anthem more than they stand for it. They wear BLM T-shirts so often during warm-ups, that it's now included in the latest version of video games. And in case you missed it, not to throw it in our faces too much, Black Lives Matter is also painted across all NBA courts.

All this woke virtue signaling is a far cry from the power of American sports in the past. And, unfortunately, the wokeness keeps winning.

Let's get into it:

For starters, how about this national anthem/Black Anthem nonsense? "The Star-Spangled Banner" became our official national anthem in 1931 and has been played at MLB games since WWI and at NFL games since WWII. The National Hockey League plays the national anthems of the US and Canada together when teams from both countries are playing each other, in both countries.

Time and time again, athletes in the past of all colors have worn red, white, and blue, and time and time again, proved that in America a person's talent and hard work are more important than a person's background. Your last name can't save you when it's all determined inside the lines. Individual achievement and identity, not identity politics, determines success. Want some examples?

How about Jesse Owens winning four gold medals in Berlin at the 1936 Olympics? Hitler and the Nazis hung their banners, chanted their slogans, and threw around all the racist rhetoric garbage about how the Aryans were the superior race. But, after the gun fired and the race started, Owens won and humiliated Adolf and the boys on their own turf. What did Jesse Owens do when "The Star-Spangled Banner" played? He saluted.

How about Sammy Sosa running out onto Wrigley Field carrying an American Flag before his first home game after the attacks of September 11? And what did Sammy do when he hit a home run in the second inning? He circled the bases proudly carrying the red, white, and blue in his hands to deafening applause from the crowd.

Personally, I've been to every major sporting event you can think of. Seriously, you name it, and I've covered it live—World Series, NBA Championships, Stanley Cup Finals, US golf and tennis tournaments, pro-bowls in Honolulu. I've had a great sports career, and the highlight of it all was being at Superbowl XXV (as a fan) when the Giants beat the Buffalo Bills and Whitney Houston sang the most perfect rendition of the national anthem you will ever hear. There wasn't a dry eye in the house. Even tough-guy players like Lawrence Taylor and Bruce Smith were tearing up. Seventy thousand fans in the seats that night, everyone waving their American flags screaming, "U-S-A, U-S-A," and there was nobody taking a damn knee. There was nobody yelling and screaming that they're being treated like a slave while they're making millions of dollars a year. There was none of that bullshit. It was a great moment, and it was the national anthem.

For me, that moment was as good as it got, so don't tell me that the national anthem before the game can't provide unity and patriotic emotion and make for a fantastic event, because it does. Now it's been ruined, and networks can't afford to show it.

So, how does the once proud National Football League play into this? Well, they were among the first of the big four (NFL, NBA, MLB, NHL) to fold to the woke mob when they announced the playing of "Lift Every Voice and Sing" to accompany "The Star-Spangled Banner" before each game.

In case you didn't know, "Lift Every Voice and Sing" is the "Black national anthem." (On a side note: if you believe there are even ten people in the entire country, white, Black, or brown, who know even a single verse of that song, then as the old saying goes, I have a bridge in Brooklyn to sell you.)

Here's a little background about this American classic: "Lift Every Voice and Sing" was originally a poem written in 1899 by James Weldon Johnson, a school principal and civil rights activist in Florida. In those days, the lynching of Blacks was a reality in the segregated South. The lyrics to the song recount the suffering of slavery and are partially intended to garner sympathy and support from the white public. Sympathy and support are what they got from Roger Goodell when he stated, "We, the National Football League, believe Black lives matter...Without Black players there would be no National Football League."

Yeah, I guess that's true in the sense that close to 75 percent of NFL players are Black. It's understandable that the league would have to at least appear to be sensitive to social justice issues as a business decision to maintain a working relationship with the players and their union. But playing a Black national anthem before games? Someone needs to tell the commissioners of these leagues that American Blacks aren't a nation. They're one of many demographic groups within this country, as are Latinos, whites, Christians, Jews, Muslims, men, women, young, old, rich, poor. Should all these groups and demographics have national anthems played before the start of games?

The Black population of America is roughly 13 percent. Latinos are roughly 20 percent. Should they have an anthem too? A national anthem shouldn't divide us. It should be all inclusive and honor our country.

In my opinion, when some of these athletes protest what they perceive to be racial injustice by taking a knee before a sporting event, they disgrace the American flag and the national anthem that celebrates it. Are these guys not aware that the "Stars and Stripes" was carried into battle by White and Black Union soldiers during our Civil War that ended slavery?

The conversation isn't only limited to athletes. Even in the military, you'll find some soldiers that will come out and say, "I was out there in Afghanistan, I was in Iraq, and I put my life on the line so that you have the opportunity to kneel." However, most of the guys I've talked to, like Joey Jones, for example, who served honorably and lost limbs in Afghanistan, he says it breaks his heart when he sees American multimillionaire athletes kneeling during the national anthem.

Like every other issue, this is one divided across political lines. There's no question that most left-leaning individuals have no problem with the wokeness, the kneeling, and the Black anthem. In fact, they encourage it and think it's long overdue, while right-leaning individuals feel the complete opposite, that it's divisive and insulting to our country and institutions. I get it.

So, do the fans have a say in any of this? Sure, they do. Bernie and I take a hundred calls a day from angry fans saying, "They're playing a Black national anthem? I'm not watching the games anymore!" and, "The players are taking knees? I'm not watching the games anymore!" Do the fans have a say? Yes! Does it matter? No! Not for the NFL it doesn't. The NFL is different from all the other leagues in that it's bulletproof. Why? One word: gambling.

Let's look at the facts:

An estimated 45.2 million Americans plan to wager on the 2021 NFL season in some form, up 36 percent year over year, according to the American Gaming Association (AGA).

The NFL has embraced legalized sports betting since the Supreme Court overturned a federal law that forbade states from authorizing legalized betting on college and professional sports in 2018. The influx of sports betting and gambling operator partnerships and advertising is expected to bring in more than $270 million in revenue for the NFL this season.

At least $12 billion will be bet on the NFL this season, according to sports betting market tracker PlayUSA.

That uptick comes as legal sports betting continues to spread across the US following the 2018 Supreme Court decision that struck down a federal law that forbade states from authorizing legalized betting on college and professional sports.

Twenty-six states and Washington, DC, now allow legal sports wagers—eight more states than at the start of last season. In addition, several states including Arizona, Connecticut, Florida, Louisiana, and New York have also approved legislation in some form but have yet to allow betting platforms to launch, potentially teeing up wagering being offered by the time the season concludes with the Super Bowl in February.

The NFL, once so staunchly against legalized sports betting that it joined other US leagues in suing New Jersey to stop legalization in 2012 with Commissioner Roger Goodell raising integrity concerns, has slowly reversed course since the Supreme Court decision. While the NFL in April 2021 became the last of the four major US professional sports leagues to sign partnerships with sports betting operators, it now has seven: Caesars Entertainment, DraftKings, FanDuel, FOX Bet, BetMGM, PointsBet, and WynnBET. Those partnerships allow those operators to purchase NFL advertising and media inventory as well as use NFL logos for retail and online sports betting. The NFL is now allowing sports betting commercials to air during game broadcasts, although it will limit broadcasters to showing six sports betting commercials per game. Stadiums in states with legal sports betting can also have betting lounges; however, only online betting is permitted as no in-person wagers are allowed.

That has led to a financial boom for the league. The NFL expects to generate roughly $270 million in revenue from sports betting and gambling deals and is projecting the category to be worth more than $1 billion within the decade, according to the *Washington Post*. Individual teams are also benefiting. The New Orleans Saints signed a twenty-year, $138 million naming rights deal with Caesars to rename the Superdome, while teams from the Arizona Cardinals to the New York Jets have signed deals with companies such as BetMGM and Fubo, respectively, for stadium betting lounges.

Fantasy football is a whole other animal. DraftKings reported that it had $298 million in revenue in its second quarter, up 320 percent year over year. The company also increased its 2021 revenue guidance from $1.21 billion to $1.29 billion.

Betting with online sportsbooks is expected to see the largest growth among wagering methods this NFL season, according to the AGA, with more than 19.5 million people placing bets online, up 73 percent year over year. In comparison, 10.5 million people are expected to place a bet at a physical casino sportsbook this season, up 58 percent year over year.

The most popular way to bet remains casually with friends, with 21.7 million expected to do so this season, an increase of 31 percent year over year. An estimated 14.6 million people will participate in a paid fantasy contest or another type of pool competition, up 69 percent from 2021, while 6.7 million are expected to place bets with a bookie, up 13 percent year over year.

In total, Americans have legally wagered nearly $27 billion on sports in the first seven months of this year, generating more than $350 million in federal, state, and local taxes.

I once got in a heated argument with Stephen A. Smith about this issue. It got pretty nasty, to the point where we didn't talk for a couple of years because I said to him, "The entire reason why the NFL is bulletproof is the gambling. There are tens of millions of dollars riding on every game, from personal bets to fantasy leagues. The NFL is run by gambling. Every Wednesday in the *New York Post*, they put out injury reports. Why does Irving in Brooklyn need to know if the left-tackle on the Patriots is injured? I live in New York, I'm a Giants fan, I've got the NFL package and can watch the Chargers play the Raiders at four o'clock. Do you think I give a shit who wins? No, I got a thousand on the Raiders like every other football fan across the country!"

He said, "Well I never bet."

I said, "Good for you, but that's very anecdotal. I'm talking about the majority of folks. I'm talking about numbers. Not you!"

We didn't talk until two years later when he came on my show in Miami and apologized for being naïve and admitted that I was right.

Bottom line: the wokeness bullet isn't penetrating the NFL as long as the league is safely cloaked in the Kevlar vest of gambling.

The NBA? Not so much.

Before we go into detail about the disgrace the NBA has become, I want to quickly touch on the disaster Major League

Baseball is descending into. Besides the ridiculous changing of the name and logo of the Cleveland Indians, which I mentioned above, Major League Baseball also shit the bed when it came to the 2021 All-Star game.

Remember when the MLB All-Star game was must-see TV? In 1980, more than 36 million people tuned in. In 2021? A laughable 8.24 million, making it the second-least-watched All-Star game in history. This is a ridiculously low number considering the game showcased one of the best lineups in years, one that included Los Angeles Angels' Japanese sensation Shohei Ohtani, who was the first player in All-Star game history to be a starting pitcher and bat lead-off, and the game's first two-way starter dating back to 1933. In other words, for the Ohtani factor alone, the numbers should have landed at least above the 10 million mark, but they clearly fell short. If you're looking for a reason, look no further than the backlash baseball received for moving the All-Star game out of Georgia to Colorado due to Georgia's new voting laws.

Not surprisingly, Colorado's early voting law actually has a smaller time window than Georgia's, clearly displaying that Major League Baseball didn't do its homework before pulling the game out of Atlanta. Maybe MLB commissioner Rob Manfred read too many tweets portraying the new law as racist? Of course, Biden jumped on the boycott-Georgia bandwagon as well, falsely stating that the law ends voting hours so working people can't vote.

"What I'm worried about is how un-American this whole initiative is. It's sick. It's sick…deciding that you're going to end voting at five o'clock when working people are just getting off work," Biden said to reporters at his first press conference on March 25, 2021. That claim was met with no pushback or scrutiny from the few reporters chosen to ask questions in the room at the time. "Among the outrageous parts of this new state law, it ends voting hours early so working people can't cast their vote after their shift is over," Biden continued.

The *Washington Post* fact-checker correctly awarded Biden its worst judgement, "Four Pinocchios," for lying to the American people.

Bottom line: the MLB and Manfred panicked and packed up to move the game from Atlanta's Truist Park to Coors Field in Denver. Wokeness won the day. Touch 'em all, Manfred! Another grand slam of utter stupidity!

Now, back to the NBA.

At one point, not so long ago, more than any other sport, basketball showed us a path forward on race relations in this country, by individual achievements that made us see past skin color. For example: Bill Russell, the Hall-of-Fame center for the Boston Celtics in the 1950s and '60s. Sure, he heard racist taunts from fans, but, on the court, he won five MVP awards, eleven championships, became the first Black coach of any major professional sports team, and was the first to win a championship.

In the 1980s, when the rivalry between Magic Johnson and Larry Bird heated up and took the nation by storm, the fans and the media often saw what they perceived as a Black-versus-white racial struggle. But the two players themselves never did. In fact, they constantly rebuffed attempts to make their rivalry about anything other than basketball. Through athletic competition, these two legends, one Black and one white, formed a unique bond based on mutual respect that transcended any racial divide the media and fans attempted to force on them.

That's ancient history now. Once a great proving ground for the power of a color-blind equality, basketball now more than any other sport (yes, even more than the NFL) appears to be more focused on promoting certain political causes than producing a watchable product for fans, undermining the great strides in racial progress made by players of past generations.

Now, LeBron James, the best basketball player the league has seen since Michael Jordan, has made more news for his comments on "systematic voter suppression" than for his performance on the court in recent years. The openly woke left-wing tilt of the NBA is also affecting LeBron's showbiz aspirations off the court. James's new *Space Jam* film reboot made less than $100 million worldwide, compared to Michael Jordan's original, which made over $230 million. The film was an embarrassing flop for someone who is consistently rated among the most famous athletes in the world.

It's also no surprise the ratings for the NBA have plummeted over the last few seasons. Nearly 40 percent of respondents in a new Harris poll said they were watching less basketball because: "The league has become too political." The poll also found 34 percent of Republicans say they "actively follow" the NBA, compared with 48 percent of Democrats—the largest such gap in any sport. Despite what ESPN and the liberal media want you to believe, the numbers show that fans just aren't crazy about the new activist woke NBA.

Speaking of ESPN, what a joke they've become. Their programming, which has widely become known as MSESPN or WokeCenter, has been hitting unprecedented ratings lows, the lowest in the history of the network. The entire channel has become more left wing than MSNBC and CNN combined over the past few years. The result? Viewers, many of whom were willing to watch the channel even during a pandemic disaster with limited sports to consume, have abandoned it in droves. How bad was it? We're talking full on crisis-mode level awfulness. ESPN had a subscriber decline of 6 percent in 2020—the largest decline ever posted—and has seen a ratings collapse, ranking 19th among the top TV networks falling behind HGTV and the Hallmark Channel.

The. Hallmark. Channel.

Look, there are many serious things going on in our country right now, and the vast majority of sports fans know where to find news about those serious things. That's why cable news ratings have skyrocketed. But fans clearly don't want their sports commentators to be weighing in on non-sports news on sports networks. The ratings show us that. How much worse can it get? That just depends on how much more WokeCenter we get and whether anyone at ESPN can regain the controls.

To their credit, ESPN has given the boot to a few of their most outspoken leftists who would rather tell you what a horrible person you are for not agreeing with them on social justice issues than reporting on anything that has to do with sports, such as: Jemele Hill, Michael Smith, and Dan Le Batard. The only question that remains is whether ESPN can revert to a more sports-focused, politically neutral version of itself, or whether its progressive bent has become baked into the network like other American institutions.

It's not only ESPN. Sports reporters and commentators lean left way more even than political journalists and commentators. One analysis put Democrat to Republican supporters at twenty-seven to one. When you think about it, those numbers should be reversed. If you add NASCAR, the biggest audience for sports, by far, is middle-aged men who politically lean right more than just about any other demographic.

In other words, the sports reporters and journalists that you watch on TV and read online or in newspapers every day have the complete opposite political ideology of the people (you) whom they're reporting to. In fact, they probably mock you. Look no further than that first-class schmuck, Keith Olbermann.

So, is sports reporting a dead or dying enterprise? No. It's just turned to shit. Why? Because it's woke.

SID-IZEN SUGGESTION

Listen, do I like this woke bullshit in sports? No. Am I going to keep watching? Of course, I am. Same reason why I hate De Niro's politics but won't let that stop me from watching *The Irishman.*

Don't let these assholes dictate the terms on what you like and don't like. If you like and support the Yankees or Mets or Giants or Jets (maybe not the Jets—remember how they screwed with little Sidney Rosenberg?) keep watching and supporting them.

If you don't like the kneeling or the alternate anthem, don't listen to it. I know I won't be. I'll put the game back on after the commercial break when that bullshit is over with. I'll still be tuning in every Sunday. Why? Because, like I told Stephen A. Smith, I have a grand on the Chargers/Raiders game…like everyone else.

CHAPTER SEVEN

THE DONALD

This might come as a surprise to some of my listeners, but until about 2012, I had absolutely no interest in politics. Zero. At that point, I was already forty-five years old, and up until then, my whole life was sports and entertainment. I didn't have any major understanding of the political world outside of what you'd read in the headlines. If Reagan got shot, I knew about it. If there was a Gulf War, I knew about it. If Clinton liked to play with cigars and interns, I knew about it.

Aside from general awareness, I had very little grasp of politics, which is why it seemed so unlikely that four years later, in 2016, I would get a job working for WABC radio in New York (a political station). Now it's my job to make politics just as relevant in my life as sports and entertainment. And I love it!

Although I love the guy now, when Donald Trump glided down that gold escalator to formally announce his candidacy on June 16, 2015, I, like many people, thought it was a joke, nothing more than an extensive publicity stunt. Nobody thought he had a chance of winning, including myself.

Friends would attempt to convince me I was wrong, saying, "He's got the right policies! He's got the right ideas! He's sick of Democratic rule! He's the guy!" Especially Bernie. I was down in South Florida, and Bernie was still on with Imus in New York, but Bernard would be a frequent guest on my show, and he'd be singing Trump's praises. I'd say, "I can't take him seriously! I just can't!" In fact, I didn't vote for Donald Trump in 2016. Even though I couldn't stand Barack Obama and didn't like Hillary Clinton (not even a little), I just thought Trump had one of the most sophomoric and dumbest campaigns I'd ever seen. Ever.

He'd stand up on stage and say he's going to build a wall while sporting a stupid red hat and giving all his opponents ridiculous nicknames. I just thought: This freaking guy is going to run the country?

But…but…it only took a couple of months after he was elected for me to realize that I was wrong. Most people would never admit that. They're so dug-in; either you love him or hate him.

I was wrong, and I told him that when he came on the show with Bernie and me. I said, "President Trump, although I've known you for a very long time," (we first met when he was a guest on my boxing show when I was in south Florida working with Scott Kaplan, twenty years earlier), "I didn't vote for you. But I have to tell you, you're doing a great job!"

Then, towards the end of the interview, after he and I and Bernie discussed everything from the White House Correspondents' Dinner to the Mexico and China deals, he said, "You know, Bernie, my favorite part of that interview was that I got Sid to come around." That's the type of guy he is. He loves the fact that he made me a believer. And he did!

Trump wasn't a politician; he didn't really know how to speak like a politician, and maybe I put too much stock into that. I came to realize when he was president that I don't want another damn politician! That's what Barrack Obama was, and he was great at it. He was eloquent, but he was full of shit and did nothing.

Early on, I fell into that trap. After a while, I stopped caring about his tweets and started caring more about the fact that the economy was in excellent shape. I loved that he crushed the ISIS caliphate. I loved his relationship with Israel, which was important to me as a Jew. I really cared about that. I love that he came through on everything from moving the embassy to Jerusalem to recognizing the Golan Heights as a part of Israel as well as not giving money to Hamas and the Palestinians. His policies were right up my alley.

Additionally, when COVID broke, who knows how many people would have died, maybe millions, if he hadn't stopped travel in from China (as the media like to label it: "The China Ban"), which he never gets credit for. Back then, the Democrats called him xenophobic and racist. But, in the end, he did some really good things that improved the lives of all Americans. Want a few examples?

America gained seven million new jobs—more than three times government experts' projections.

Middle-class family income increased nearly $6,000—more than five times the gains during the entire previous administration.

The unemployment rate reached 3.5 percent, the lowest in a half-century.

Signed the Tax Cuts and Jobs Act—the largest tax reform package in history.

More than six million American workers received wage increases, bonuses, and increased benefits thanks to the tax cuts.

For the first time in nearly seventy years, the United States has become a net energy exporter.

The United States is now the number one producer of oil and natural gas in the world.

Illegal crossings plummeted over 87 percent where the wall has been constructed.

First president to meet with a leader of North Korea and the first sitting president to cross the demilitarized zone into North Korea.

Killed Soleimani (an Iranian general responsible for countless attacks against American and allied troops in Iraq and Afghanistan).

That's a few out many of his accomplishments he should be remembered for.

Election Night 2016

I was in Washington, DC, the night of the election. My wife, Danielle, was being sworn in the next morning at the Supreme Court (she's an attorney and can now try cases in front of the Supreme Court). It was a huge honor. We stayed in a fancy hotel, and I remember seeing all these people walking around like zombies, basically crying, and I thought, Holy Shit! This guy is gonna win!

The next morning, when the show started, I was in DC and Bernie was in New York. We had literally spent the whole year of 2016 fighting—worse than Mike and the Mad Dog, worse than Hannity and Colmes. We'd been yelling and screaming at each other. He loved Trump, and I thought Trump was a moron.

But I went on the air and said, "Let me tell you something, whoever the president is, I need him or her to do a good job because I have two little babies, and this country needs to be healthy. I didn't vote for him. I didn't like him, but you know what? Today, I want him to do well!"

Bernie was shocked. "Oh my God, really? I thought we would be at each other's throats."

From that day on, I gave Donald Trump a chance, and because I gave him a chance, I ended up becoming a big supporter and voted enthusiastically for him in 2020 and would do so again if he decides to run in 2024.

Trump VS the Media

Let's face it. If you combine all the social media platforms (TikTok, Instagram, Facebook, Twitter, and so on) with the overwhelmingly leftward tilt of "mainstream" media outlets (ABC, CBS, NBC, CNN, MSNBC, *New York Times*, *Washington Post*, and so on) you couldn't come to any conclusion other than Donald Trump was treated worse than any other president in history. Sure, the Democrats and the media hated Reagan, both Bushes, and some people say the Nixon years were the worst, blah, blah, blah. But no one was treated more poorly or more unfairly than our 45th president.

That same bullshit media coverage continues. As this book is being written, Trump has been out of office for over a year, yet you can put on MSNBC at any given hour of any given day and find any given anchor blaming Trump for any little thing: "It's cloudy with a chance of rain in Cleveland this afternoon…. Clearly, Trump's climate change policies are to blame for this possibility of inclement weather!"

I remember the Sunday morning before the 20th anniversary of 9/11, turning on liberal media outlets, and every one of these morons was blaming the Afghanistan debacle, which was clearly Joe Biden's fault, on Trump. Yes, Trump brokered a deal with the Taliban. Yes, Trump announced a plan to pull out all American forces from Afghanistan. However, the failed execution of the pull-out followed by the embarrassing military defeat is 100 percent Biden's fault. The guy got caught with his pants down and his Depend diapers twisting in the wind for all the world to see.

The media busted Trump's balls every day he was president, and they continue to bust his balls every day he's been out of office. It's ridiculously unnecessary and unfortunately all too predictable. But that's how they make their living, especially MSNBC and CNN.

Guys like Chuck Todd (a dear friend of mine for many years, especially during the worst times of my life) have been completely irrational when it comes to Trump. This is why Trump Derangement Syndrome (TDS) is real, folks. There's no question about it. Some of the smartest people I know turn into complete lunatics. Even Jake Tapper, who has moments where he's lucid and seems like he knows what's going on, will suddenly say something incredibly idiotic, like last May when he commented on why he's hesitant to give GOP officials airtime on his show:

"If they're willing to lie about Joe Biden wanting to steal your hamburgers, and Qanon and the Big Lie about the election, what are they not willing to lie about?" Tapper said. "Why should I put any of them on TV?"

Now, there's nowhere to go. Fox News used to be the place, but they added a bunch of left-wing talking heads like Harold Ford Jr. and Donna Brazile, and that's become difficult to watch. Not that any news outlet is 100 percent down the middle, but if you want someplace to go that's not going to bash Trump or the GOP at every turn, all you really have now is Newsmax. They do a good job, but it's just not enough.

Even the current network nightly news anchors are a joke: Lester Holt, David Muir, Norah O'Donnell. All of them. When I was a kid, the network anchors were Peter Jennings, Tom Brokaw, Dan Rather—they were all liberals, but they were so professional at their jobs that you really couldn't tell where they personally stood on most of the issues they were reporting on.

These folks now are just so blatantly obvious in their hatred of Trump and Republicans that even when they try to appear objective, it doesn't come off that way. So, you have your *World News Tonight* shows at 6:30 p.m., your local news at 11 p.m., and your cable news channels running 24/7. All of them, all of them, are way too biased in their reporting, which is incredibly irresponsible and a disservice to anyone tuning in.

Election Night 2020

I remember watching CNN the night of the 2016 election, and as the results were pouring in, seeing John King and Wolf Blitzer scrambling to figure out whether there was still a way

Trump could mathematically lose the election. That didn't happen. I stayed up until 3:30 a.m. to watch Donald Trump make his acceptance speech in the ballroom of the Hilton hotel on 6th Avenue in midtown Manhattan. I didn't sleep at all that night.

On election night of 2020, I was home and fell asleep. At the time I went to bed, Trump was up. He was winning in all the major states. I woke up and went to work at 5 a.m., and Bernie and I started the show playing "We Are the Champions" by Queen because we thought Trump had won.

Was the election rigged? I'm not going to go that far. I don't know. Many people contend that it was rigged even before election night with the way the media treated Donald Trump and the way the media and most of the public ignored the Hunter Biden scandal, which was reported on a month before the election by Tucker Carlson, and nobody paid attention to it, except a handful of reporters, one of whom was Miranda Devine of the *New York Post*, who I believe is the best writer in the country. Her recent book about Hunter Biden's corrupt and sleazy existence is more evidence of that.

Different things were happening before the election that would make you believe that the media, for the most part, helped rig it because they refused to present a lot of the negative information about Joe Biden and his family to the public. For example, it was not until December 9, 2020, more than a month after the election, that the media felt safe to report on the FBI investigation into Hunter Biden. And that was only because he issued a statement himself confirming its existence.

The media blackout worked. Trump pollster John McLaughlin found that 36 percent of Joe Biden voters were unaware of the entire saga, and that 4.6 percent of total Biden voters would have changed their minds if they had known about it, clearly enough to swing the election in key states.

I do think 1,000 percent that there was some monkey business going on and, in the end, Trump probably got screwed, but I'm not ready to say that it cost him the election. I'm just not going to do that because if I do, and if he runs and wins in 2024, then I have to take the side of "Well they're going to say it was rigged too." And then the never-ending cycle of doubt, division, and bullshit continues to go round and round.

Trump and January Sixth

My big problem with what President Trump did that day was not the speech he gave to his supporters on the Ellipse, because he did say (I think once was not enough), "Walk peacefully to the Capital." My big problem was that he waited too long to do anything about it, and that was the wrong decision. I think he did a terrible job that day. It's not worthy of wasting taxpayer dollars on congressional investigations, that's ridiculous, but to say he did nothing wrong that day is silly too. He screwed up. It was not a good day for Donald Trump and not how his presidency should have ended.

However, to put things in a different perspective, there were many a night in Seattle, Portland, Chicago, Atlanta, New York, and in many other cities across America, during all the BLM/Antifa riots, that were much worse than anything that occurred at the capital. More civilians got hurt, more cops got hurt, more damage to property was done, businesses were burned, and more deaths occurred.

Is it wrong to compare the incidents through a political lens? In my opinion, no. I don't think so. Here's why: Do you remember any prominent left-wing politicians condemning the riots? The looting? The burning of businesses? The constant disrespect for law enforcement? No. It didn't happen. Joe Biden, when asked about the nightly riots in the streets, answered, "Rioting is not a form of protest." Could he be any more tame in his response? Way to calm the chaos there, Captain America.

A House GOP member commented: "You can moan and groan, but he [Trump] was far more explicit about his calls for peace than some of the BLM and left-wing rioters and politicians were this summer when we saw violence sweep across this nation." I completely agree with that statement. Another GOP official said, "Trump has held over six hundred rallies in the last four years. None of them included assaulting police, destroying businesses, or burning down cities."

Another thing I find comical is how the left defines what happened on January 6th as an "insurrection." That is not what we saw on January 6th, which was a rally that turned into a melee that turned violent. Ashli Babbitt died that day, and the liberal media didn't give a shit about her. They're still lying to this day about the cop who died (of natural causes). He wasn't killed by a crazy Trump supporter with a fire extinguisher.

As of December 2021, nearly fifty individuals who participated in the "insurrection" have been sentenced. Some misdemeanors, some felonies. Is that going to satisfy the media and political left? Absolutely not. The House committee has been lining up Trump administration cohorts from former political strategist Steve Bannon to former chief of staff Mark Meadows to publicly testify under oath to what, if anything, was Trump's involvement. Because that's who they're really after: Trump.

Can he be prosecuted? Some say yes, others say no. Can he claim executive privilege? Some say as a former president he has that right; others say since he's out of office that privilege no longer protects him, and it would be up to the sitting president in office to grant.

All I know is, whatever happens going forward, our country will continue to be divided. There's no immediate answer to our current national chasm. Grab your popcorn, folks. This is going to be a long and messy chapter in our history.

Let's talk numbers about the "Insurrection."

A full two-thirds of Republicans don't consider the January 6 events at the Capitol to have been an attack on the US government.

A Quinnipiac poll found that 66 percent of Republicans do not view the storming of the US Capitol, or as the left called it, "an insurrection," as an attack on the government.

The poll also found that the vast majority of Republican voters don't hold Trump responsible for the events of that day, regardless of whether it was an attack on the government; 21 percent of Republican poll respondents said that Trump had "not much" responsibility for the storming of the US Capitol, while 56 percent said he had no responsibility for it whatsoever.

If you look at the ongoing congressional investigations into what happened that day, 74 percent of Republicans said that enough is already known about the events of January 6, compared to just 38 percent of Democrats and 58 percent of independent voters who said the same.

The poll's results tell us that Republican voters have largely moved on from January 6, and some GOP candidates have taken the same path.

Look at this number: 51 percent of Americans told Quinnipiac that they believe Trump has been undermining democracy since the 2020 election ended, though significant partisan divides exist on this question. For instance, 94 percent of Democrats said Trump was undermining democracy, while 85 percent of Republicans denied that, saying he's in fact protecting democracy. In other words, folks, our nation has never been more divided since the Civil War.

Among the public overall, 48 percent say that the criminal penalties those who broke into the US Capitol have been receiving are not severe enough, while two-in-ten say they are too severe, and 29 percent say the penalties are about right. Democrats are far more likely than Republicans to say that the penalties are not severe enough.

An overwhelming majority of Democrats (71 percent) say the criminal penalties are not severe enough, while 21 percent say they are about right. Just 6 percent say the penalties are too severe.

Republicans are more divided in their assessment of the criminal penalties. About four in ten Republicans and Republican leaners (38 percent) say that the penalties for those who broke into the Capitol are too severe. A nearly equal share (39 percent) say the penalties are about right. Only 19 percent of Republicans say that the criminal penalties are not severe enough.

There are also ideological divides among Republicans: 44 percent of conservative Republicans say that the penalties for those who broke into the Capitol are too severe, while 28 percent of moderate and liberal Republicans say the same. Moderate and liberal Republicans are twice as likely as conservative Republicans to say that the penalties are not severe enough (28 percent vs. 14 percent). There are no significant ideological divides among Democrats.

Since March, the share of the public that says there has been too little attention paid to the January riot at the Capitol has risen by 8 percentage points (35 percent now, 27 percent then), while there has been a comparable decline in the share saying it is receiving the right amount of attention. Nearly three in ten (29 percent) say there has been too much attention to the riot and its impacts, little changed from six months ago.

Democrats account for much of this change. The share of Democrats saying there has been too little attention paid to the January 6 riot and its impacts has increased fourteen points since March (from 40 percent to 54 percent).

A 57 percent majority of Republicans say that there has been too much attention paid to the January 6 riot, roughly on par with March. In the current survey, 65 percent of conservative Republicans say the riot and its impacts have gotten too much attention, compared with 41 percent of moderate and liberal Republicans.

Liberal Democrats are somewhat more likely than conservative and moderate Democrats to say that there has been too little attention to the January 6 riot and its impacts (60 percent vs. 49 percent).

Look, we could talk numbers until the cows come home. In the end, half the country is going to believe one thing, and the other half is going to believe another thing, 50 percent certain that the other 50 percent is dead wrong. Well, there's one thing I'm 100 percent certain I'm right about: no matter what our differences, we're still Americans and live in the greatest country on the planet. I'm damn proud of it and so should you be!

Twitter Ban

"Free Speech has been taken away from the President of the United States because the Radical Left Lunatics are afraid of the truth, but the truth will come out anyway, bigger and stronger than ever before. The People of our Country will not stand for it! These corrupt social media companies must pay a political price and must never again be allowed to destroy and decimate our Electoral Process."

That was Donald Trump's statement when he was banned from Twitter. And I completely agree with him. Why did they do it? Plain and simple: they hate President Trump. He spent four years exposing the media for what it really is to the American public. They couldn't stand him. Now Jack Dorsey has stepped down as the CEO of Twitter, but it's not going to matter because the next person in line is going to be just as bad as Jack, so at the end of the day they just wanted to shut Trump up. And you would think in America, something like that couldn't happen—but it's happened.

When you consider the fact that the Taliban, who are responsible for countless American lives (men and women) during that ridiculous exit out of Afghanistan, orchestrated by Joe Biden, They're on Twitter, along with people like "Hawk" Newsome, the leader of BLM. Race baiters like Louis Farrakhan are on Twitter and other social media, and to a lesser extent, those liberal politicians who actually encourage people to commit violence.

For example, you had people like Maxine Waters, a congresswoman from California, telling followers to walk up to Republicans in restaurants and harass them:

"Let's make sure we show up wherever we have to show up. And if you see anybody from that Cabinet in a restaurant, in a department store, at a gasoline station, you get out and you create a crowd. And you push back on them. And you tell them they're not welcome anymore, anywhere."

And she's not the only one. When you look at the people, from terrorists, to murderers, to race-baiting politicians, who are allowed to be on social media—even Ayatollah Khomeini, the Supreme Leader of Iran, has a Twitter account—and yet President Trump is banned from those same platforms? That tells you all you need to know about how sick our society is.

Trump the New Media Mogul?

As has been speculated for a while, the Trump Media & Technology Group is working to launch a social media app called "Truth Social" early next year. Can you blame the guy for trying?

According to reports: "Mr. Trump announced plans to launch Truth Social earlier this year, saying it would allow conversation without discrimination on the basis of political ideology."

He's still the voice of over seventy million Americans. He needs to get back out there and talk to his supporters and continue to relay the message he wants to get out.

If you're not watching Fox News or Newsmax, or not listening to *Bernie & Sid*, you're not aware of just how horrible Joe Biden is. What is the state of our country at the moment? Inflation, wide-open borders, Russia and China becoming stronger every single day.

When you look at the first fourteen months of Joe Biden's presidency—and I was around for Jimmy Carter—I don't think it's hyperbole to say that he is the worst president in the history of the United States, and I wouldn't even limit it to him: his whole cabinet; Kamala Harris, if she's not the worst VP in history, then I don't know who is. She was put in charge of one thing: the border, and that's been a complete disaster. She giggles about it.

Possible Future Legal Trouble?

I have never paid much attention to Donald Trump's businesses. Honestly, I don't think the general public does either, but the Manhattan DA's office has been trying to nail him with something, anything, forever, whether it was his taxes or his businesses dealings, for the better part of the last few decades.

It's gone nowhere with Cy Vance, the outgoing Manhattan DA, and it will go nowhere with the new DA, Alvin Bragg. No one cares. It's gotten to the point with me, and I think most people, that the legal system has dug so deep into Trump's past that now it's now become the boy who cried wolf.

Let's put the cards on the table right now. If it was Eric or Donald Trump Jr. who lived the lifestyle that Hunter Biden has lived his whole life, you'd never hear the end of it. They tried to legally go after Donald and his kids. They're all good kids. Hunter Biden smoked crack, had babies with strippers, banged his dead brother's ex-wife. He's got deep dealings with China and other countries for hundreds of millions of dollars. This guy is a "lowlife." If that was any one of Trump's kids, you'd never hear the end of it.

2024

Is Trump going to run again? I believe he will. If he decides to run again, I think the field of potential candidates should step aside and clear the way. This is still Trump's party, for better or worse.

At last year's CPAC Convention during a straw poll that included President Trump and all other potential candidates, Trump won by 55 percent. His second closet opponent was Ron DeSantis, governor of Florida, who got 21 percent. In fact, DeSantis was the only other GOP potential candidate who reached double figures. Without Trump in the poll, DeSantis wins.

Now, as he gears up for another run, he still has to deal with the ramifications of the 2022 midterms. If you look at what's currently going on in Georgia, and other states, where Donald Trump felt like he was either betrayed or abandoned by GOP officials, he's now handpicking loyalist candidates to primary the sitting GOP officials he felt did him wrong.

Does this smell like revenge, or is it the right thing to do?

I think it's a bit of both. There's no doubt that the loss in Georgia stung Donald Trump in a big way, although I think he did a lousy job of supporting those folks in Georgia. I really do. And that's part of the reason why a guy like Warnock, who is not a very good guy or candidate, won. That's the bottom line. Ossoff, too.

So, there is a revenge factor here for Trump. I think he knows he dropped the ball. I also think he knows that Georgia needs better GOP candidates, like Herschel Walker. Brian Kemp, the sitting governor, who turned out to be very wishy-washy and was perceived to be stabbing Donald Trump in the back for not questioning the state's election results, is now squarely in Trump's crosshairs. In fact, he already handpicked a primary opponent to oust Kemp. If there's one thing that we know about Trump, which Kemp is now finding out first-hand, is that Trump doesn't forget or forgive very easily.

Look, in my opinion, Donald Trump was a great president. His policies were spot on, and if he decides to run in 2024, I will enthusiastically campaign for and vote for him.

If he could ever find a way to win again and calm down with the outbursts and the name-calling and getting into non-sensical arguments about shit nobody cares about, he could be the greatest president ever, and that is saying a lot. That's a huge statement, but he's got to recognize that and act on it. Otherwise, he's just going to go down as an effective, loud-mouth, one-term president.

However, there is definitely an opening for Trump should he decide to throw his red MAGA hat back in the ring. Joe Biden isn't doing himself any favors. In fact, every day that goes by, he just proves how incapable he is of carrying out the tasks of the presidency. Inflation through the roof, gas prices through the roof, crime through the roof, and now a possible World War Three scenario with the Russian invasion of Ukraine.

Come on, do we really think this would be happening if Trump was still president? I don't. Neither do most people.

According to *The Hill*: "A new Harvard Center for American Political Studies (CAPS)-Harris Poll survey released Friday found that 62 percent of those polled believed Putin would not be moving against Ukraine if Trump had been president. When looking strictly at the answers of Democrats and Republicans, 85 percent of Republicans and 38 percent of Democrats answered this way."

Another poll from HarrisX echoes the Harvard poll: 58 percent of voters blame Biden's policies for the Russian invasion, while 42 percent blame Trump's policies. Among independents, the people who ultimately decide many elections, 66 percent blame Biden while just 34 percent blame Trump.

To peel the onion further, here are some easy questions to ask if you take away all the usual distractions that the mere mention of the names "Trump" or "Biden" provides to any conversation from a partisan perspective:

Did Putin invade any neighboring countries when Trump was in power from January 2017 to January 2021? (Answer: no.)

Did Putin annex any neighboring countries when President Obama was in power prior to Trump? (Answer: Yes—Putin annexed Crimea in 2014.)

Yet here we are, almost fourteen months since Trump was in the Oval Office, and he's still living rent-free in the minds of those who get paid to talk about world affairs on TV. And as usual, there's a disconnect between them and the public.

Here are some facts:

—Under Trump, ISIS went from one of our top threats during the Obama years to almost nonexistent. The ISIS "caliphate" in Iraq and Syria was destroyed. Attacks and beheadings of Westerners stopped. ISIS became an afterthought.

—Under Trump, North Korea went from carrying out regular missile tests over or near neighboring countries, including Japan, and regularly threatening to obliterate the US, to being relatively well-behaved beyond its borders. It stopped missile tests for eighteen months, from late 2017 to mid-2019, and it dialed-down its reckless rhetoric. Not a perfect result, but an improvement from the Obama-Biden years.

It should be noted that President Obama also initiated the infamous US-Russia "reset," complete with a big red "reset" button that then Secretary of State Hillary Clinton handed to her Russian counterpart, Sergei Lavrov.

And it was Obama and Biden who mocked then Republican presidential nominee Mitt Romney for declaring that Russia was our biggest geopolitical foe during a presidential debate a decade ago.

"The 1980s are now calling to ask for their foreign policy back. Because the Cold War has been over for 20 years," Obama declared during that October 2012 debate. "But Governor, when it comes to our foreign policy, you seem to want to import the foreign policies of the 1980s, just like the social policy of the 1950s, and the economic policies of the 1920s."

Biden, during a 2012 campaign rally, said, "I think it's fair to say when it comes to Russia, based on only what we know he's said so far, Governor Romney is mired in a Cold War mindset," which viewed the world "through a Cold War prism that is totally out of touch with the realities of the 21st Century."

Here's what the New York Times said about Romney's worldviews in 2012: "Mitt Romney still considers Russia to be America's 'No. 1 geopolitical foe.' His comments display either a shocking lack of knowledge about international affairs or just craven politics. Either way, they are reckless and unworthy of a major presidential contender."

Uh-huh.

As CNN's Chris Cillizza remarked on Twitter about the Obama-Romney exchange of a decade earlier: "What looked like a major flub during the 2012 campaign – and was used as a political cudgel by Obama – now looks very, very different."

So why did Putin wait until now to invade Ukraine?

It's hard not to connect a dot back to the deadly debacle of the US withdrawal of Afghanistan last August. The Biden administration was caught completely flat-footed when the Taliban took Kabul far faster than anyone on Team Biden expected. It got infinitely worse when images were broadcast around the world showing Afghans hanging off of US airplanes, trying to escape. The killing of thirteen US service members by an ISIS-K bomber after we handed security over to the Taliban was the final blow that marked a downward spiral for President Biden.

Chuck Todd believes Putin would have invaded Ukraine even if Trump were president. But former United Nations ambassador Nikki Haley sees it differently.

"What I will tell you about President Trump is, as much as everybody wants to talk about what he says, what I look at is what he did," Haley told Todd on *Meet the Press*. "He sanctioned Russia. He expelled diplomats. He shut off Nord Stream 2, which is all Putin ever wanted. He built up our military. And he made us energy independent. All of those things countered Putin and countered Russia. This never would have happened under Trump."

Hard to argue with any of those points.

This is all ultimately irrelevant, of course. Hypotheticals aren't helping brave, resilient Ukrainians in their fight against Russia—and it doesn't matter which president or ex-president is to blame.

What matters is what happens moving forward and hitting Putin where it hurts. And that starts with the US becoming more energy independent again. Asked, "In light of Russia's attack on Ukraine and soaring gasoline prices, should the Biden administration ease its focus on climate change and allow more oil and natural gas exploration in the US or not?" Sixty-nine percent of respondents said "yes," including a majority of Democrats.

But President Biden, who shut down the Keystone XL pipeline less than 24 hours after taking office and then suspended drilling leases in the Arctic National Wildlife Refuge, isn't budging.

To do that would mean to admit error—something that is a foreign concept in this administration.

SID-IZEN SUGGESTION
. . . .

Look, I know everyone is pretty much dug-in on their personal feelings, thoughts, and opinions of Donald Trump. It's hard not to be. If you're a supporter, I say stay on the train and see where it takes him. Maybe back to Washington in 2024?

If you're less than enthusiastic about Trump, then maybe after reading this you'll think about giving him another chance. Just like I did. After all, as 45 once said, "What the hell do you have to lose?"

CHAPTER EIGHT

HOW TO DESTROY A CITY IN TWO WORDS: LIBERAL POLICIES

F olks, what happens when liberal mayors and district attorneys get soft on crime?

You guessed it! YOU GET MORE CRIME.

These days, nobody owns softness on crime quite like liberal Democrats. Shall we peruse the laundry list of horrible policies being enacted from coast to coast in this country?

Where to start?

Efforts to "defund the police."

Prosecutors who won't charge criminals unless they hit a high threshold of crime.

Re-categorizations of some truly monstrous offenses from felonies to misdemeanors.

"Zero bail" and "no cash bail" policies.

A revolving door judicial system, where criminals can go from the street to prison to court and back out on the street within a few short hours.

And there are even elected Democrats in government who have literally proposed that we eliminate federal prisons. You can't make this stuff up! And you shouldn't be surprised at the inevitable results:

In liberal-run cities like Los Angeles and San Francisco, district attorneys publicly announced that theft of merchandise valued under $1,000 will not be prosecuted. Well, to nobody's surprise, there are now organized waves of smash and grabs all over those cities, where mobs of criminals are literally walking out with $999 or less of stolen goods, never to be prosecuted.

Meanwhile, Philadelphia, the City of Brotherly Love, is on track for over five hundred murders this year, a 55 percent increase versus pre-COVID levels. Other cities like Baltimore, St. Louis, and Detroit are reporting similar increases.

Chicago, a big liberal mecca, is a dumpster fire. They're likely to surpass one thousand murders this year with spikes in other crimes as well. Their mayor is on television essentially blaming businesses for the crime surge, while the great men and women of the Chicago Police Department had to cancel a portion of their regularly scheduled time off for their officers in order "to address current crime patterns."

But if you really want to examine how liberal policies enacted by liberal mayors and district attorneys literally destroy cities, look no further than the Big Apple, my home-town, the once great city of New York.

There's no question about it! The golden age of New York city was from 1993–2013, a great twenty-year run that lasted through five consecutive terms of GOP/Independent mayors—two under Rudy Giuliani and three under Michael Bloomberg.

When Bloomberg had to leave office due to term limits, we knew this overwhelmingly Democratic city would deliver us a left-wing nut job who would reverse all the progress made over the previous two decades. "Tough on crime" and "low taxes" were out the goddamn window. A storm of shit was ominously approaching, and there was nothing we could do about it. This storm had a name, and that name was Warren Wilhelm Jr., otherwise known as Bill de Blasio.

De Blasio's tenure as mayor of New York City is thankfully over and done with, but it is worth examining how he and his left-wing policies dismantled the foundations of the city's decades of success. Studying de Blasio's tenure can give future mayors across the country a road map for doing things differ-ently—meaning better. Understanding New York's recent his-tory can also help provide the city with a long-term direction.

A resurgent Gotham would send a powerful message of confidence, nationally and internationally. Looking closely at the de Blasio years can help expose not only what the mayor did wrong but also what should be done to reverse the city's slide.

The mayoral tenures of Rudolph Giuliani and Michael Bloomberg were successful for one overarching reason: both leaders focused on the first priority of government, the rule of law. Ensuring citizen safety and maintaining order led to significant and sustained reductions in crime. During the early 1990s, when David Dinkins was mayor, New York City was suffering from more than two thousand homicides a year. Criminals, as well as the law-abiding, knew that the city had a decidedly unsafe feel. The high crime rates and menacing atmosphere discouraged tourists, investment, business development, and newcomers.

When Giuliani won the 1993 election, he, together with his first police commissioner, William J. Bratton, resolved to apply groundbreaking policing strategies. The strategies (some of which started under the tenure of Police Commissioner Raymond Kelly in 1992) included a renewed focus on data to determine where crimes took place—especially via CompStat, a computerized system, introduced by Bratton, that tracked crime by neighborhood and held local precinct commanders accountable. They also included bolstering the department's anti-crime unit, which pursued known criminals more aggressively. And the NYPD put into action a "broken windows" policing approach that cracked down on aggressive panhandling, the notorious "squeegee men" who menaced drivers coming into Manhattan, and subway fare-beaters, who were often found to have committed other crimes as well. This comprehensive effort helped initiate a city-saving 80 percent crime drop over the next few decades. Mayor Bloomberg maintained these approaches and accelerated tactics like stop-and-frisk to get guns off the street.

By contrast, de Blasio took a more skeptical view of the police. He campaigned on ending stop-and-frisk. He spoke openly of warning his biracial son, Dante, about interacting with the police. And, while he had hired Bratton to serve a second stint as head of the NYPD, de Blasio seemed to encourage protests against the cops following the police-related deaths of Michael Brown in Ferguson and Eric Garner in New York in 2014. When, in the aftermath of those protests, two New York City police officers, Rafael Ramos and Wenjian Liu, were murdered at point-blank range as they sat in their patrol car, Police Benevolent Association head Patrick Lynch told the press: "There's blood on many hands tonight. That blood on the hands starts at City Hall in the Office of the Mayor." Hundreds of police officers turned their backs on the mayor at Liu's funeral.

After this strong message from the men and women on the front lines of the fight against crime, de Blasio tried to moderate his progressivism, at least on law and order. He reaffirmed his desire to "put an end to economic and social inequalities that threaten to unravel the city we love" but admitted that doing so depended on keeping the streets safe. He toned down his criticisms of the police. According to the *New York Times*'s Dana Rubinstein, the Ramos and Liu backlash proved "a turning point in the de Blasio administration, making the mayor more eager to accommodate the department." Few ever mistook de Blasio for a police lover, and it took the deaths of two of New York's Finest to drive home the obvious point that a mayor should not make enemies with his or her police force.

Then came the coronavirus. De Blasio was a COVID-19 skeptic in the pandemic's early stages. In February 2020, he admonished people not to avoid Asian neighborhoods, saying, "New York City's Chinatowns are open for business!"

His health commissioner, Oxiris Barbot, added: "While it is understandable for some New Yorkers to feel concerned about the novel coronavirus situation, we cannot stand for racist and stigmatizing rhetoric." Though de Blasio should have known better, by March he was still complacent in the face of the threat. On March 5, after New York governor Andrew Cuomo had issued a stay-at-home order, de Blasio told New Yorkers to go about their business—even as he faced a near-revolt from his health department.

According to Lawrence Wright's *The Plague Year: America in the Time of Covid*, the health department complained: "Every message that we want to get to the public needs to go through him, and they end up getting nixed. City Hall continues to sideline and neuter the country's premier health department." Another official complained of the mayor: "He doesn't get it. He's not convinced there's a volcano about to blow beneath us." In the end, New York City was devastated by the virus, logging more than one million cases (every one in eight people) and more than thirty-five thousand deaths.

As the pandemic continued, New York's underlying problems worsened. Following the George Floyd protests in the spring of 2020, de Blasio took the slogan "defund the police" seriously and pledged to cut $1 billion from the police budget and reduce the size of the force by 1,100. It didn't take a genius to predict the inevitable outcome: crime exploded, burglary surged 42 percent, car thefts rose 67 percent, and shootings nearly doubled, leading to a 44 percent rise in homicides.

New York residents rated crime as the number two issue of concern in an April 2021 poll, trailing only the pandemic. Adding to the sense of dissolution in the city was the growing presence of the homeless in public spaces—not just on street corners but in parks and other public facilities, as well as on transit systems. Like other worsening problems that affected everyday life for New Yorkers, however, the homelessness issue did not seem to trouble the mayor in the slightest.

On education, always an issue of high importance in the city, de Blasio proved as divisive as he was ineffective. His vision of educational equality appeared to mean closing off alternative pathways for kids in New York City's poorly performing traditional public schools, where a majority of African American and Latino students don't score at grade level in math or reading. Parents understandably sought other options. To no one's surprise, de Blasio obstructed their efforts. He had a particular aversion to charter schools. Though charters are public schools—albeit ones that often get much better results and thus have long waiting lists of parents clamoring to get their children in—de Blasio tried to make charters pay rent to the city, as if they were private-sector entities.

In his anti-charter efforts, de Blasio often found himself impeded by former (now disgraced) New York governor Andrew Cuomo, with whom he had a relationship of mutual disdain. De Blasio had actually worked for Cuomo at Housing and Urban Development during the Clinton administration, but that did not stop them from becoming mortal enemies later on. The *New York Times*'s Shane Goldmacher and J. David Goodman wrote that the two men were "engaged in a feud so nasty, petty and prolonged that even in the cutthroat politics of New York, few can remember ever seeing anything quite like it."

Lots of politicians have rivalries, but the Cuomo-de Blasio feud would have implications on the everyday lives of the citizens of New York. In 2015, Cuomo even shut down the subways in anticipation of a winter storm without warning de Blasio, and he mocked the mayor's haphazard plans for closing Rikers Island prison. The two Democrats fought over de Blasio's efforts to thwart charter schools until late in the mayor's second term, when Cuomo faced his own problems—political fallout from his mishandling of the COVID-19 crisis, along with several sexual harassment accusations, which led to his resignation.

De Blasio also sought to eliminate the tests for New York's elite schools, such as Stuyvesant and Bronx Science. These public schools, which base admissions strictly on entrance exams, have long been a ticket to a better life for children from lower-income and immigrant families. The insistence on the exam as the sole criterion ensured that every child who made it felt that he or she belonged in the school and could compete in the high-level classes. Alleging that the schools' standards produced unfair demographic outcomes, de Blasio tried to stop their reliance on the merit-based test. Fortunately, de Blasio was thwarted in these efforts as well.

De Blasio's other main foray into education policy came in his cooperation with teachers' unions on keeping public schools closed longer than necessary during the pandemic. Private schools and public schools elsewhere figured out how to manage the COVID threat, but de Blasio seemed uninterested in doing so. Since the teachers' unions were among his main political benefactors, he was generally willing to collaborate with them against public school parents.

For all de Blasio's bluster about equity, the results of his educational policies were abysmal. The racial achievement gap worsened during his tenure. Enrollment in New York City's public schools plummeted from nearly one million to fewer than 890,000 students. Half of the city's public schools have seen an enrollment drop of at least 10 percent since 2017, reflecting parental interest in exploring other options for their children. Some of those options were private schools in the city, but others represented a more dramatic choice: an exodus from de Blasio's increasingly unlivable city.

Stories about departures from New York did not start with COVID-19. Census figures for 2018 demonstrated significant out-migration from the New York region, which led the nation in that category. New York's high cost of living was a factor, with rents skyrocketing even in the outer boroughs. COVID just accelerated the inevitable departures.

Bloomberg News reported a doubling of people looking to leave the city. A Manhattan Institute survey revealed that only 23 percent of Bronx residents said that they were happy with their neighborhood, and 26 percent of Staten Islanders reported an interest in moving "somewhere far away from New York City."

United Van Lines reported a serious disconnect in New York-linked long-distance moves: 70 percent were made by people leaving the state, while 30 percent were people coming in. Rents dropped 7.8 percent in the third quarter of 2020, and office vacancy rates approached 20 percent. Hedge funds closed their New York operations and headed for sunny (and tax-free) Florida.

Everyone seemed to have stories of people who had left. Yet, while 1.4 million people reportedly had moved out of the New York metro area since 2010, the census revealed that New York's population had actually grown relative to 2010, to 8.8 million—an increase of more than six hundred thousand from the previous decade. De Blasio, of course, took credit for this development, crowing on Twitter: "The Big Apple just got bigger!" What a schmuck!

One factor in the population increase was the Department of City Planning's addition of 265,000 previously missing housing units, which city officials explained as part of an effort to improve the count. City demographer Arun Peter Lobo told the *New York Times*: "This allowed the Census Bureau to enumerate half a million people which they would have otherwise missed." Look, of course you want to get the best possible count, but the move raises the question of whether population comparisons from the beginning and the end of the de Blasio term are apples-to-apples comparisons.

Regardless, New York will need the maximum number of citizens to maintain the tax base required to support de Blasio's blowout spending. Municipal unions were rewarded for their support with gushers of taxpayer dollars. De Blasio boosted spending by $25 billion, an astonishing 34 percent increase, almost quadruple the inflation rate of 9 percent over that period. The budget crunch precipitated by COVID did not slow down his spending either. From spring 2020 through summer 2021—the peak of the pandemic—New York City's back payments to teachers totaled $1.5 billion.

Under de Blasio, New York's debt increased by $40 billion. To put that in perspective, this $40 billion growth is the equivalent of approximately 40 percent of New York's bloated current budget. New York has a history of carrying unmanageable levels of debt—most prominently in the 1970s, during the Abe Beame administration. Back then, an $11 billion debt threatened to push New York into default, and President Gerald Ford refused to rescue the city without the promise of significant fiscal reforms. The crisis prompted the legendary *Daily News* headline "Ford to City: Drop Dead" and epitomized the depths to which the city had fallen in that period.

Today, de Blasio's debt—vastly larger—threatens the city once again, though it will be his successors who have to deal with it. Whatever solutions they come up with will have to consider that New York is already the nation's most heavily taxed city, with a tax burden 90 percent higher, on average, than other large American cities. Increasing that burden to deal with the debt crisis risks driving out more New Yorkers, further eroding the tax base.

De Blasio and his disastrous liberal policies also helped drive away New Yorkers by making it clear that he disfavored certain populations. His most prominent target was Orthodox Jews. An upsurge in hate crimes against the Orthodox community did not lead him to direct more police resources, or even strong rhetoric, to address the problem. But he came down hard on the Orthodox—and here, he did call for more police—for violations of his COVID-19 protocols.

This is not to say that there were not protocol violators in the Orthodox community; there were. But violators in other communities seemed not to attract the mayor's ire as much. De Blasio had police weld shut park gates in Orthodox neighborhoods and send out officers to monitor compliance by Orthodox institutions. In a tweet, he even called out Jews by name, saying, "My message to the Jewish community, and all communities, is this simple: the time for warnings has passed. I have instructed the NYPD to proceed immediately to summon or even arrest those who gather in large groups. This is about stopping this disease and saving lives. Period."

Former Democratic congressman Max Rose responded: "For him to paint the entire Jewish community as uncooperative was breathtaking. Words matter. Threatening every Jewish New Yorker with arrest was beyond insensitive."

Asians had their problems with de Blasio too. He appeared to avoid visits to Chinese neighborhoods, and he didn't make his first appearance at a Chinatown Lunar New Year parade until 2019, well into his second term. In August 2020, he turned his back on an Asian American bakery manager suffering under COVID restrictions, saying, "We're all hurting." Hate crimes against Asians rose during de Blasio's tenure, especially during the pandemic, when, according to NYPD statistics, they exploded by 1,300 percent. De Blasio wasn't personally to blame for these racist attacks. In my opinion, his weak policies were, but many in the Asian community felt that he was not doing enough to stop them.

In a March 2021 vigil for victims of anti-Asian hate crimes, protesters chanted, "What are you going to do about it?" as de Blasio spoke. When the mayor went to leave, they surrounded his motorcade. Asians had their problems with de Blasio's education policies too, but their protests that his moves against merit-based testing would hurt low-income members of their community, and cut Asian elite-school enrollment in half, fell on deaf ears.

De Blasio also created the impression that he didn't much like taxpaying, law-abiding, business-running New Yorkers either. Journalist Seth Barron felt that this was a deliberate strategy to shape the electorate that de Blasio desired. As Barron wrote in *The Last Days of New York*, "[Only people] who tolerate the politics of racial resentment, onerous business regulations, and a school system dedicated to equity over excellence stick it out." Despite a 72 percent disapproval rate in June 2021, de Blasio was doing okay with the people who mattered to him. "He's only a failure by the standards of the 90 percent of the city who want to have a livable city with economic opportunity, good schools, and safe streets."

Bloomberg and Giuliani attacked the mayor's job with passion and dedication, but de Blasio had a questionable work ethic, showing up late, finding time to go to his gym in Brooklyn (at taxpayer expense) for two hours nearly every day, and even engaging in a pointless run for president, in which he barely registered with Iowa voters. As Edward-Isaac Dovere wrote in *Battle for the Soul*, at one Iowa rally, "A little under three dozen people came to see de Blasio that day. More people tended to show up to protest him at rallies back home." Near the end of his tenure, the mayor would take long, aimless walks, and New Yorkers being New Yorkers told him what they thought of him. "No one wants you," a man with his young son screamed at de Blasio, in a scene chronicled by Politico. "You're the worst. YOU'RE THE WORST!" Got to love New Yorkers.

I never thought de Blasio appeared to like his job, the city, its residents, or even, as a Red Sox fan, its sports teams. He treated New Yorkers accordingly, making their city less safe, less livable, less fiscally sustainable, and less united.

With the de Blasio years finally over, will the new guy, Eric Adams, who positioned himself as a moderate in relation to the extreme progressives in the Democratic primary, be any better? I mean, he can't be any worse. Can he?

Personally, I think Adams is a phony. I think he plays very well to whatever audience he's in front of at any given time. He was a cop for twenty plus years, so at least crime is an issue he's familiar with, and crime is most certainly the number one issue to deal with right now. Bo Dietl, who's a frequent guest on our show, once said these are the three biggest problems in our city right now: crime, crime, and crime. Bo is a guy who wants to fight crime and supposedly so does Eric Adams. Still, Adams also subscribes to all the other bullshit liberal positions that attract him to the left-wing voters of the city. So, he knows how to appease both sides, and I don't trust him.

He's a very good politician, and that's why he crushed Curtis Sliwa (the GOP mayoral nominee) at the polls—that and the overwhelming numbers in which Democrats outnumber Republicans in New York City. Still, I don't think Adams is the answer. Just as I don't think Hochul is the answer as governor. I think she's Andrew Cuomo 2.0, and I think Eric Adams is basically Bill de Blasio 2.0. Adams will be a little tougher on crime than de Blasio was but not a huge ideological difference there, unfortunately.

Still, I hope Adams does a better job than I think he will do. I could be wrong. I was wrong about Donald Trump. Maybe, just maybe, he'll come in and do a tremendous job and fix this city. Only time will tell.

I believe that any governor, mayor, and district attorney's primary focus, ambitious as it sounds, should be nothing less than ensuring public safety and in a way, de Blasio offers a template for all elected officials across the country of how to achieve this: just do the opposite of what he did. Such an approach would include backing the police, spending less on giveaways to municipal unions, supporting charter schools and elite public schools, treating all citizens as equals and maintaining a strong work ethic. A rejection of de Blasioism and left-wing policies implies the very agenda that could help bring back every once great city in this country and possibly around the world.

SID-IZEN SUGGESTION

Look, with all the bullshit that I just laid out, New York is still the greatest city in the world. There's no energy like in New York City. The restaurants are the best, and for me, there's still nothing like going to a game at Madison Square Garden.

For the record, I'm not telling anyone to leave New York. I'm not telling anyone to leave any state, city, or town you're currently living in. Those are personal decisions everyone has to make on their own.

For me? I'm staying. I'm fighting. As for de Blasio and all failed liberal policies, you can get the hell out. And don't let Lady Liberty hit you where the sun doesn't shine on your way out of town!

✪   ✪   ✪

So, what are some policies your local mayor or district attorney can implement to decrease crime and improve quality of life to tax-paying citizens?

For starters, bring back stop-and-frisk. Many law enforcement experts I've talked to tell me that those who benefit most from stop-and-frisk are law-abiding minorities. And anyone who is stopped and frisked who hasn't committed a crime has nothing to fear. The anti-crime policy "stop, question, and frisk" (popularly known as "stop-and-frisk") saves innocent lives and removes guns from the rough streets of America's cities.

Remember when audio from then New York City Mayor Mike Bloomberg surfaced in which he enthusiastically endorsed stop-and-frisk? Angering leftists, the ex-Republican said, "Ninety-five percent of murderers and murder victims are male, minorities, sixteen to twenty-five, in virtually every city." It's true that minority males, and particularly young Blacks and Hispanics, are more likely to be arrested for, and convicted of, crimes than whites. Some such arrests are wrongfully perpetrated by racist law enforcement officers; in most instances, disciplinary actions are rightfully taken. However, many Democrats condemn stop-and-frisk as "racial profiling."

Maybe it is. Yet, those who benefit most from stop-and-frisk are law-abiding minorities, as Department of Justice statistics show that minorities, particularly poor ones, are far more likely to be victims of crime than others. And anyone who is stopped and frisked who hasn't committed a crime has nothing to fear.

Stop-and-frisk as a public safety measure has been proved by objective statistics and attested to by former New York City police executives and mayors. A RAND Corporation study of New York stop-and-frisk data concluded, after considering arrest rates and the races of criminal suspects, that there was no evidence of racial discrimination. But tell that to the pro-perpetrator, leftist agitators who infest today's Democratic Party.

Since 1968, cops throughout America have made "Terry" stops, so called because of the US Supreme Court decision *Terry v. Ohio*. Under *Terry*, "reasonable suspicion" that a crime is being committed, or has been, justifies such stops.

Even if stop-and-frisk constitutes racial profiling, it's legal, as the US Supreme Court ruled in 1975's *United States v. Brignoni-Ponce*. Unanimously, the justices decreed that what is now called racial profiling is acceptable, legitimate, and legal. They decided that the "likelihood that any given person of Mexican ancestry is an alien is high enough to make Mexican appearance a relevant factor" for the US Border Patrol and other law enforcement entities to stop vehicles and question the occupants regarding their immigration status. Writing for the court, Justice Lewis Powell said that "a heavily loaded vehicle," "an extraordinary number of passengers," and/or "the characteristic appearance of persons who live in Mexico," could, in concert, warrant such stops.

But this billionaire Bloomberg, a former Democratic would-be president, condemns stop-and-frisk now, and apologizes for it, after crediting it for saving "countless lives." He's brought a wallet to a gunfight and focused attention on an issue that hurts Democrats. Bloomberg has sold out. He knows that not repudiating stop-and-frisk means any future political prospects in the new Democratic "woke" party will immediately come to an end, much like his growth spurt during puberty. (He's a little guy.)

Former New York Police Department spokesman Paul Browne says stop-and-frisk "saves lives, especially in communities disproportionately affected by crime, and especially among young men of color." Former New York police commissioners Ray Kelly and Howard Safir, and ex-Mayor Rudy Giuliani, all agree.

The *Washington Post*'s liberal columnist Richard Cohen told NPR's *Talk of the Nation* host Neal Conan that stop-and-frisk is highly effective and lowers violent crime. Conan added that stop-and-frisk is somewhat "problematic," as higher percentages of Blacks and Hispanics get arrested than whites.

That's true, but unbiased studies consistently prove that nonwhites are more likely to commit violent crimes than whites. What's truly problematic for the Democrats is that by ignoring the truth and facts, and caving to identity politics, most likely voters could perceive their party as pro-perp. And if that happens, their candidates for office outside the bluest of blue districts will be doomed.

Here's another liberal policy that needs to go the way of the dodo bird and Rosie O'Donnell's dietary plans: bail reform.

Let's face it; bail reform measures come as a slap in the face to police who work hard to keep communities safe and earn the public's trust. If a violent offender is put back onto the streets, the safety of everyone in that neighborhood is called into question. Seeing an arrested person walk free makes people doubt the legitimacy of the police officer who arrested that person, which leads to further distrust and skepticism of police. It also creates a sense of fear within the community and heightens tensions among neighbors when they believe that the criminal justice system is not working effectively.

Bail reform changes directly relate to what former attorney general William Barr has described as a growing disrespect for law enforcement. "Police officers must look on as the criminals that they have risked their lives to apprehend get turned loose by 'social justice' DAs and 'progressive' judges who no longer see their role as protecting the community from predators," Barr wrote in the *New York Post*. "Some DAs have even exposed police officers to greater danger by announcing that they will not prosecute those who resist police."

Thankfully, New York's residents have seen the problems with bail reform and are beginning to express their frustrations. According to a poll conducted by Siena College, 59 percent say that that bail reform is bad for New York. Only 33 percent of respondents said the new law is good for New York. Those numbers represent a complete reversal since the law was announced in April 2019. At that time, 55 percent of residents said it was a good thing, while 38 percent said it was bad.

Want a real-life example on how liberal bail reform kills innocent people? Want a real-life example how this issue is a problem everywhere in this country and not just in big cities? Here's one from Harris County, Texas:

> Daniel Munsterman was a devoted son and caretaker to his 87-year-old mother who suffered from Alzheimer's. Caitlynne Rose was a young mother and was 8 months pregnant. Gregory Brooks had a wonderful sense of humor, but he prided himself in taking his education seriously and was proud to be one of the first in his family to go to college. Reginald Larry was on his way to his grandmother's house when he stopped to get a drink at a corner store.
>
> What do Daniel, Caitlynne, Gregory and Reginald have in common? All four of them were murdered. The suspects were all released on multiple bonds by Harris County Judges in the past year. And sadly, there are many more. (As reported by Crime Stoppers.)

It's ridiculous that public safety is placed at a higher risk when career habitual offenders are continuously released back to the community despite being charged with multiple violent crimes. Misdemeanor judges are bound by a Federal Court ruling basically removing cash bail for most misdemeanor charges, district judges who handle felony cases are not. When a defendant out on felony bond is arrested on a new felony charge, the judge then has discretion whether or not to revoke the original bond or grant them a new bond giving them the chance to return to the community once again.

Time and time again, we're seeing the same defendants released on multiple bonds, continually being arrested for additional felony crimes and yet are still getting out of jail on new bonds. What's the problem with that? Ask the families of Daniel, Caitlynne, Gregory, and Reginald and many others whose loved ones have been murdered by defendants out on multiple bonds, people who have shown their propensity to thumb their nose at the law.

Which leads to a series of questions that every community deserves answers to:

How many felony defendants are out on repeat multiple bonds and for what types of offenses?

How many felony defendants are in bond forfeiture and have been declared fugitives?

How many defendants committed crimes after a motion to revoke the original bond was denied?

How many defendants have actually had their bonds revoked after being charged with another crime while out on bond?

How many of our citizens have become crime victims as a result of offenders violating their conditions of bond?

The defendant charged with capital murder in the slaying of Byron Handy was on felony probation and yet managed to be granted three separate bonds for offenses, all involving the use of a firearm. His bond was not revoked, and inexplicably he was allowed to remain on probation. The defendant charged with the slaying of Matthew Franklin was out on bond for three charges of aggravated robbery with a deadly weapon and aggravated assault. The defendant wanted for the murder of Reginald Larry was released on multiple felony bonds including murder and two aggravated assault charges. He was on deferred adjudication while all this occurred yet was allowed to remain in the community. The defendant charged with two counts of capital murder in the deaths of Kevin Kelly and Sylvernia Edwards was out on multiple felony bonds at the time of their killings.

I could go on and on with examples like the above, which happen in every community, in every city, in every state, in which innocent citizens paid the ultimate price for liberal criminal justice and bond reform measures. It's no easy task to explain to family why a loved one was killed. It simply defies logic. What do you tell the family of an eleven-year-old boy who was shot by a defendant already out on multiple bonds for murder, evading arrest, and unlawfully carrying a weapon? How do you try to put into context what is happening to our criminal justice system to families who are grieving and searching for answers as to why their loved one was murdered?

Public safety is at a higher risk when career habitual offenders are continuously released back into the community. Everyone who supports criminal justice and bond reform should be demanding as much information as possible to determine which measures are working and which are putting the public at risk. Increasing crime rates detrimentally affect all of us. Improving public safety must be a non-partisan issue.

SID-IZEN SOLUTION

NOW IS THE TIME TO ACT.

Given the decline in public support, now is the time for the public and law enforcement officers to come together in opposition to bail reform and put pressure on legislators to overturn the law and restore safety and justice to our communities affected by it.

Take a stand to help your community fight for the respect we all know they deserve. Speak out against bail reform and send messages of support to families that are dealing with its impacts.

Together, we can work to overturn this disrespectful law that's putting our communities at risk.

CHAPTER NINE

SID-IZEN LIVES MATTER

Anyone else miss the old days when "BLM" stood for Bureau of Land Management?

I'm so sick and tired of these "rioters" disguised as "activists" and the politicians and talking heads on TV who provide support and political cover for criminal behavior that does nothing but deepen the racial divides in this country. For instance, take this schmuck Roland Martin, who goes on any channel that will allow him on, and talks about how the biggest problem this country faces is white supremacy and white supremacists.

White supremacists? Really? Where? Point them out! I haven't seen or heard anything about people clad in white hoods going out killing scores of Jews and Blacks. Have you? No. And I'm Jewish.

Here's a cute little story: A few months ago on the corner of 96th and Broadway on the Upper West Side of Manhattan, there was a group of old white-haired Jewish people holding signs that said "White supremacy kills" and "Stop killing Black people." I walked over to these people holding the signs, and I said, "You know who kills Black people?"

And one of these idiots looked up at me and said, "Who?"

I said, "Black people kill Black people! Not white people! Not white supremacists! Black people!"

Look at the numbers. It's not even close. The facts are that in the Black community, there is a disproportionate amount of crime. Black males ages fifteen to forty-five, although roughly 5 percent of the population, commit 52 percent of violent crimes in this country. We have to start having a conversation not about how white people treat Black people but how Black people treat Black people and why that community continues to be riddled with crime issues.

If you want to blame white people, then tell me how? What are we doing? Because all I see is one specific community that is having a very difficult time policing themselves, one specific community having a difficult time trying to stop killing themselves, and one specific community having a difficult time producing more and more successful people, and that's a fact. Until we have that conversation, nothing is going to change.

Jason Whitlock is a well-known Black journalist, known to many sports fans from his work at ESPN, until they showed him the door the second he showed signs of not being an uber-liberal. Jason is now speaking out against Black Lives Matter, calling it a "cleverly marketed slogan that provides cover for extremists to undermine racial progress and bully American citizens to support Democrat politicians.

"Despite the sweet-sounding name, Black Lives Matter acts as a racial divider, no different from the KKK." Whitlock said, "Black Lives Matter and Antifa serve as the modern-day 'enforcement arm' of the Democratic Party."

When asked in a recent interview to expound on his take comparing Black Lives Matter to the KKK, Whitlock said, "The Ku Klux Klan was founded on Christmas Eve 1865 by Confederate soldiers dedicated to undermining the racial progress sparked by the Civil War and Emancipation Proclamation. It was at night when the KKK took part in terrorist raids against Blacks and white Republicans. They used intimidation, destroyed property, assaulted and killed in an effort to influence upcoming elections."

"Black Lives Matter and Antifa protests have primarily terrorized and destroyed property in Black communities at night," he wrote. "BLM and Antifa have attempted to intimidate white Republicans. BLM protests have been violent and caused the assassination of law enforcement officers and other citizens."

Whitlock said he believes it is not a coincidence that "Black Lives Matter riots pick up during an election cycle and disappear after the votes have been counted." He says his analogy comparing the KKK and Black Lives Matter is "not far-fetched, nor is it hard to comprehend particularly for the mainstream media.

"My analogy is far more substantive and accurate than pretending the events at the Capitol on January sixth were an armed insurrection analogous to Pearl Harbor and 9/11," he said. "Black Lives Matter, founded by self-described trained Marxists, has a stated goal of disrupting Western Civilization traditions and values."

I wholeheartedly agree with Jason.

Now take "celebrity activists" like John Legend and Chrissy Teigen and Roland Martin. These people are danger-ous because they have public platforms. They have fans and followers, and people who react to their views on politics. But these people don't talk about the real issues of crime and lack of education and lack of family structure that's going on in their communities; they just want to point the finger and blame everybody else.

They're not telling you the truth, folks! They're disingen-uous at best and bald-faced liars at worst. So, if or when (don't hold your breath) they ever want to have an honest discus-sion about the real issues facing the Black community, then maybe we could start solving a lot of the bigger problems in America today.

Do Black lives matter? Of course they do. But it is now abundantly clear that the lives, safety, and dignity of Black

men, women, and children are not really what drives organizers of the Black Lives Matter movement, and that's a
real shame.

The world has been sold a bill of goods about BLM's goals.
Now we see they are about creating civil unrest and nothing
more. We should have realized this after one of its co-founders
proudly declared she is a "trained Marxist." Marxism, by defi-
nition, "argues for a worker revolution to overturn capitalism
in favor of communism."

The BLM website says the organization "builds power to
bring justice, healing and freedom to Black people." Really?
Then why haven't they mobilized in hotspot neighborhoods
where Blacks are most frequently victimized?

In New York, BLM organizers concentrate on painting
their name on streets yet do nothing to help stop the ever-in-
creasing civilian slaughter of mostly Black citizens. Shootings
during the first six months of this year are up 46 percent,
and homicides increased more than 20 percent. Yet BLM's
cries for defunding the police continue, and the left-wing politicians' response was to cut $1 billion from the New York
Police Department budget. The department's anti-crime unit
focused on disarming criminals and curbing violent crime in
mostly minority neighborhoods was disbanded.

On what planet does that make sense? Remember when
during a hot summer night, a twenty-two-month-old baby
boy, Davell Gardner, was senselessly shot and killed at a

Brooklyn barbecue? The shooting also left three adult men wounded. All of the victims were Black, and police suspect the shooters were too. "They are talking about 'Black Lives Matter,'" Davell's grandmother said, "but Black lives don't matter because Black people are trying to kill other Black people. It needs to stop!…Catch the bastards!"

In Chicago, where more than one hundred mostly Black people were shot by civilians over a recent weekend, one local reverend said it's an "open season" killing field. And, yes, the majority of victims and known assailants are Black.

So, where is the Black Lives Matter movement in Chicago to try to curb this trend? Has BLM piled into the Windy City to marshal local ministers, community leaders, and concerned citizens to try to combat the carnage against black Americans? No.

In Minneapolis, authorities reported that at least 116 people were shot in the four weeks following the death of George Floyd. Recently, there were three gang-related shootings in one day, one in a majority-Black neighborhood in north Minneapolis where fifty children (ages five to fourteen) were at football practice. One eyewitness, a mother, posted a chilling video saying the shooters obviously had "no regard for life." Luckily, no child was shot.

Did Black Lives Matter come in to help soothe the psychic wounds of those mostly Black children or to mobilize grown-ups to guard against another incident? No.

In Atlanta, at the burned-out Wendy's restaurant where BLM gathered after police killed a Black man who shot at them with a Taser, another tragedy took place. An eight-year-old Black child was fatally shot as she rode by in a car. It was yet another mindless Black-on-Black shooting. Her father later told the criminals: "You killed a child. She didn't do nothing to nobody. Black Lives Matter? You killing your own."

The mantra of Black Lives Matter is now unfortunately a part of the American lexicon. All clear-thinking citizens embrace it and the idea that violent police tactics need to be abolished. Embracing those ideals and the BLM organization are two very different things.

The movement, funded with multiple millions of dollars donated by well-meaning corporations, celebrities, and concerned people, is fatally flawed. BLM lacks true leadership, fiscal transparency, and an explicit mission statement.

To be viable, the organization must condemn the violence perpetrated in its name, along with the illegal occupations, the burning and looting, and the vandalism so frequently seen. So far, we haven't heard a peep from their self-described Marxist leadership.

A standard bullshit excuse you'll often hear is that "the rioters" must not be compared with "the protesters." But the distinction is not as obvious as the media would like to make out. In many locations, police and fire services were diverted to accommodate these massive "protests," which in turn created a vacuum that enabled the outbreak of riotous activity.

One resident of Minneapolis explained to a reporter that emergency services told him they would simply be unavailable during the weekend of May 29th–31st, while other locals recounted with amazement that police were totally absent as their neighborhoods burned, due to allocation of essential services diverted to maintain control of "peaceful protests."

In Milwaukee, a (Black) man described being chased down by rioters after getting off the bus on his way home from work. He saw no difference between protesters and rioters; the bullshit idea that these groups can be so neatly distinguished is ridiculous.

The resulting destruction has set majority-minority neighborhoods back economically for months or years, if not longer. Most had already been struggling due to the pandemic, with the riots interrupting already tentative reopening plans. To exclude the perspectives of these people from popular media narratives amounts to a kind of purposefully moral left-wing snobbery. Talk about biased.

Even today, if you were to travel around a city like Minneapolis, Seattle, Portland, and many others, you'd frequently see the anarchist "A" symbol scrawled on charred and/ or boarded-up buildings, as well as catchphrases like "Viva la revolución"—expressions typical of left-wing activists.

Something extreme is happening in America. I could give dozens of additional examples that don't remotely align with the prevailing media narrative that has flourished in the wake of this "movement." And if you're not being told the truth, how would you ever know?

So, who are the schmucks behind the curtain who started all this chaos? Black Lives Matter founders: Alicia Garza, Patrisse Cullors, and Opal Tometi. These racist, America-hating radicals have been candid about their anti-democratic agenda, even before the #BlackLivesMatter hashtag first appeared in 2013.

Cullors, who is also a prison abolitionist and LGBT activist, has publicly stated that she and Garza were "trained Marxists," and their rhetoric is regularly shot through with explicitly socialist ideas and phrases. In 2015, Garza appeared at a "gathering" of Left Forum, which holds events with titles such as "Lenin: His Work's Pertinence Here and Now."

Garza's own panel was dedicated to the theme of "No Justice, No Peace: Confronting the Crises of Capitalism & Democracy." She told her audience that "it's not possible for a world to emerge where Black lives matter if it's under capitalism, and it's not possible to abolish capitalism without a struggle against national oppression." This was no one-off. It's part of her consistent message. "Black lives can't matter under capitalism," she told the *San Francisco Weekly*. "They're like oil and water."

In that same interview, she also chided Bernie Sanders for being weak on socialism: "It sounds like he's been talking a lot about being a Social Democrat, which is still left of where the Democratic Party is, but it's not socialism. It's democratic capitalism.... There should be more voices saying, 'This is not actually socialism, and socialism is actually possible.'" Again, this BLM founder could not have been more clear: not only is Black liberation incompatible with capitalism, but democracy is incompatible with real socialism.

Last year, Garza told Maine progressives, "We're talking about changing how we've organized this country.... I believe we all have work to do to keep dismantling the organizing principle of this society." She's also stated that "social movements all over the world have used Marx and Lenin as a foundation to interrupt these systems that are really negatively impacting the majority of people." These are all messages that plainly echo Lenin's own 1917-era admonitions to the Social Democrats who urged Bolsheviks to work within Russia's legal framework rather than simply seize power.

Cullors, similarly, reports that she learned about communism in a radical political organization she'd joined, wherein "I added the teachings and beliefs of Mao, Marx and Lenin to my knowledge." Along with Tometi (who once traveled to Venezuela to lend her support to what she calls "a fair, transparent election system recognized as among the best in the world"), she's publicly praised communist cop-killer Joanne

Chesimard, who fled to Cuba to escape prosecution (and is now apparently known as Assata Shakur). In the same 2015 clip, filmed at a #BlogHer15 event that reportedly drew almost two thousand attendees, the pair urged the audience to chant the communist slogan, "We have nothing to lose but our chains."

These explicitly stated communist sympathies have an institutional component. Garza and Cullors, in particular, have worked for groups associated with the Marxist-Leninist Freedom Road Socialist Organization. Cullors trained for years at the Labor Community Strategy Center, which Eric Mann, a former member of the Weather Underground, calls his Strategy Center the "Harvard of Revolutionary graduate schools," and sometimes, "the University of Caracas Revolutionary Graduate School."

Look, most Americans, whether Republicans or Democrats, don't want violence. BLM's Marxist roots and violent methods don't reflect mainstream progressives (or Black Americans, for that matter) any more than extreme right-wing groups reflect mainstream conservatives.

But one would not know this based on the skewed way that these groups are reported on. Surely, it is no slur on social justice or racial equality to point out that radical, often violent anti-capitalist, anti-democratic groups inspired by communist dictators do not have America's best interests at heart.

If that's something public figures aren't allowed to say for fear of insulting BLM and its supporters, then we have little hope of making a sustained and bipartisan moral case against street violence—not just in the shadow of this election but in all those that follow.

How about the hypocrisy of these anti-capitalist Black Lives Matter founders? The only color they love more than black is green. It's been widely reported that Black Lives Matter co-founder Patrisse Khan-Cullors purchased four homes in predominantly white neighborhoods in California for an estimated $3.2 million. Cullors, the "trained Marxist," is evidently no practicing Marxist herself.

Although Cullors and the Black Lives Matter Global Network Foundation hide behind both a veil of Marxism and "social justice" in qualifying efforts to encourage rioting and looting for months at the expense of national security and the American taxpayer, Cullors's decisions are representative of a capitalist.

Cullors employs doublespeak, relying on capitalism to advance herself and her business model. Karl Marx and Friedrich Engels's conception of revolt against the central banking system, among other institutions, is mirrored by the BLM mob but not the insiders raking in the benefits. The very "bourgeois," or property-owning class that the mob claims is a product of white supremacy, must only be a farce if its Black leaders are part of it.

The thirty-seven-year-old co-founder has amassed considerable wealth for someone in favor of communism. Having earned an undergraduate degree from the prestigious University of California, Los Angeles, Cullors then went on to receive a master's in fine arts at the University of Southern California.

As of today, these two programs combined will cost someone in-state an estimated $96,064. Only in America today can someone pay almost $100,000 for a degree, publish an institutionally award-winning thesis featuring "elements of performance, live music, sculpture and improvisation," and still skate by calling themselves a Marxist. These achievements are not only indicative of someone with high status but also someone seeking an individualism Marx would say leads to "misery, agony of toil, slavery, ignorance, brutality, and mental degradation."

Do not be fooled, though. This development remains part of a trend among the hypocritical BLM foundation working to undermine this country through deceptive rationale. The mob rioting and looting may seem to be inspired by Marxism, but the corporate heads running the show are woke capitalists.

The BLM Global Network Foundation financial disclosures from February show $90 million in donations. But according to several chapters across the nation in a letter penned last November, they "have received little to no financial resources from the BLM movement since its launch in 2013," as reported by the *Daily Mail.*

BLM's foundation is not tax-exempt. It is funded by many anonymous sources and notably financially assisted by left-wing 501(c)(3) charity Thousand Currents. Therefore, Thousand Currents maintains all donations, allowing virtue-signaling celebrities, politicians, and corporations who provide BLM money to perform write-offs come tax season, according to the Internal Revenue Service.

Not only is Cullors clearly living comfortably given her position, but she is providing an outlet for other woke capitalists to improve upon both their images and their bank accounts. Given the extraordinarily high tax rates for the wealthy, this is foreseeably a cushy hedge.

While billionaire George Soros, Ellen DeGeneres, John Cena, and other high-profile people, in addition to dozens of corporations, fleshed out millions for Cullors's ostensibly Marxist foundation, the virtue-signaling elites received continuous pats on the back. In turn, they all helped each other out and profited while cities burned.

It is only fitting that a co-founder of a collectivist movement would benefit so enormously from violence and unrest. Hugo Chavez, who brought socialism to Venezuela and once said it is "bad" to be wealthy, had a net worth between $1 and $2 billion by his death, as a report by the Criminal Justice International Associates confirmed.

Cuban dictator Fidel Castro had twenty homes, a ninety-foot yacht, and at one point was number seven by the metric of *Forbes* of the richest leaders across the world with a net worth of $900 million. Nicolae Ceaușescu, who from 1965 to 1989 was the dictator of the Socialist Republic of Romania, had fifteen palaces and gave his own dog a motorcade.

Surely, the BLM movement that has taken America by storm feels eerily similar to collectivist movements of the past. Black Lives Matter protesters raised their fists in solidarity as they marched in Brooklyn Center, Minnesota. In 1917, the Bolsheviks marched like so as their salute. The Communist Party of Germany stitched the clenched fist in 1924 on the badges of soldiers. In 1949, the People's Liberation Army of China marched in salute of Communist leader Mao Zedong with their fists held high.

Regardless of the collectivist-leanings of the liberal movement, what is clear is that Cullors and the deceptive BLM foundation calling the shots are categorically profiting off its unprecedented power grab in American society, and they need to be called out on it. As the public now knows, the founders of the BLM movement have been proven to be either: ignorant, complacent, or corrupt. And in most a combination of all three.

✪ ✪ ✪

Now let me touch on another batch of abject losers that go by the ridiculous name: Antifa.

Have you ever seen such a collective group of unwashed, unkempt, nerdy, green-haired, nose-ring-wearing, vegan, "social justice warriors" with no job, no aspirations, and a deep love to argue that there are more than two genders? Just a pathetic bunch.

It's amazing they have time to spew their garbage beliefs on social media. They're all over Twitter, Instagram, TikTok. Don't they have better things to do like throw a brick through the window of a Starbucks in the name of "fighting the power!"? Schmucks.

Unfortunately, socialist and anarchist groups like Antifa have created a growing online structure that serves to support violence, especially against law enforcement. Data suggests that "the appearance of posts with anti-police outrage and/or memes and coded language increased over 1,000% on Twitter and 300% on Reddit in recent months during social justice protests." In Seattle, groups with a radicalized collectivist agenda even managed to carve out a de facto autonomous zone for several weeks before it collapsed into chaos and violent crime.

Antifa's Fascist History

Over the past few years, especially since the 2016 election, Antifa has become much more prominent in some of America's biggest liberal hotspots, most notably around Portland, Oregon, and other places in the Pacific Northwest.

Portland has become a major political powder keg over the past couple of years. Maybe it's the constant gloomy weather in the area, or maybe it's something in the water, but either way, Portland has become the epicenter of political division. Antifa has played a huge role in ensuring this divide gets wider. They refuse to make their grievances known through any means other than violence.

It's been tried, but the group's leaders refuse to sit down and discuss things. The group takes an all-or-nothing kind of attitude towards their demands, and they're violent enough to follow through on their threats. There's no such thing as compromise in their world.

They don't protest, they riot. They damage property. They assault peaceful protesters. They stop the free speech of others—and don't forget that they've actively laid siege to ICE detention centers.

They should have been labeled as a domestic terrorist group a LONG time ago. But they somehow skirted underneath the radar, even while The Proud Boys, the group formed specifically to fight against them, was labeled as a hate group by the Southern Poverty Law Center.

But here we are in a very trying time in American history. The George Floyd incident has set America into a frenzy. Cities all over the country are erupting in protests that often turn to riots—but it's not for the reason you think.

Antifa actually got its start decades ago but didn't really start to show itself here in America until the Occupy Wall Street movement. They were one of the driving forces for the chaos that ensued in New York during that time, but nobody knew it yet.

At the time, no one knew enough about the disorganized organization to make heads or tails of their motives. There are videos popping up from all over showing Antifa members provoking rioting, vandalism, looting, and violence. They're not there to protest for racial equality or raise awareness of police brutality; they're there to cause chaos and wreak havoc, and we don't know what their endgame is.

Now, of course, we've all seen these cowardly masked "protesters" inciting riots and claiming its mission is to defeat fascism in the United States, but at its core, Antifa is just another anti-police movement on the rise in this country. Here are three reasons why Antifa is just another cop-hating movement:

1. Endless rambling on "police brutality" on the Antifa website.

Their attitudes toward police are on proud display in this official Antifa pamphlet distributed to members. This rambling Antifa manifesto complains that "police officers are an advance guard for a stepped-up reign of terror on Black and Latino people." This type of rhetoric is dangerous and only increases the distrust and tension between inner-city citizens and the police who protect those communities.

2. Antifa leaders calling for "dead cops."

In September, a co-founder of Antifa's Washington, DC, arm and professor at John Jay College stirred up controversy when he jeered about dead cops. Michael Isaacson proudly proclaimed on his Twitter page that he considers it "a privilege to teach future dead cops" as a professor at the school. Fortunately, his vulgar statements have been condemned by people on both sides of the aisle. However, it is deeply disturbing that individuals like Isaacson, who openly promote violent anti-police views, hold positions of authority at American universities.

3. Violence against police officers at Antifa rallies.

Almost every time Antifa hits the streets, they direct violence at police officers. Antifa demonstrators hurled smoke and projectiles at police officers during rallies in downtown Portland, injuring at least two officers. They also threw bottles of urine, cement, and Molotov cocktails at police officers at other rallies in New York, Seattle, Minneapolis, and Chicago. These instances prove that Antifa does not engage in peaceful protests. They incite riots, plain and simple. Antifa claims to have legitimate points of view, but their violent rhetoric and actions directed toward police officers makes them nothing more than an anti-police anarchist group.

So, who makes up the majority of these schmucks?

David Marcus in a recent article in *The Federalist*, wrote about Antifa and who makes up their majority:

"First of all, notice that 95% of them are lily-white and when they are arrested and the masks come off, they are mostly spoiled white punks. The funny thing is that Antifa is made up almost entirely of white fascists and yet the media tries to play them up as a diverse group and Democrats sing their praises because they criminally assault conservatives."

Antifa wears masks not because they are afraid what the law will do; as we have seen, they never pay a price no matter how serious the assault. They wear masks so mommy and daddy don't cut them off or out of their wills.

On the left, however, race seems not to matter to the media, and Antifa is a case in point. Yet race actually does come into play here, and Antifa is a quintessentially white leftist group.

"Antifa's goals are not those of most non-white Americans," Marcus points out. "Most non-white Americans don't want to destroy the systems of government, abolish the police, end capitalism, or cripple corporations. The group is absolutely trying to impose a style of anarchy that is steeped in (and almost unique to) whiteness," he writes.

The truth concealed behind the masks is essential in the case of Antifa, precisely because of the contrived image of diversity they endeavor to project.

"When cowards wear masks to engage in violence, we must remove the masks to see who we are actually dealing with—not the fairy tale of diversity version," Marcus states.

"Don't believe the progressive narrative: Antifa is mostly a bunch of privileged white dudes," he concludes.

I agree with Mr. Marcus.

SID-IZEN SOLUTION

In plain English, people who consider themselves "Antifa" or "BLM" and participate in their hateful riots are utter losers—in my opinion, of course.

Unfortunately, mainstream media and politicians too often refuse to condemn Antifa and BLM violence toward police officers. We know the vast majority of Americans support police officers. That is why we seek to provide a united voice against violent anti-cop forces like Antifa and BLM.

If you support America's police and are sick of cop-hating groups like Antifa, we encourage you to support your local law enforcement agencies. Donate resources if possible. Help defend America. The enemies are within.

I'LL LEAVE YOU WITH THIS

At the introduction of this book, I left you with one particular word that my father taught me: persistence. He didn't teach it by defining the word out of the dictionary. He taught it to me by example, by pushing me beyond where I thought my limits were. He taught me to face my fears and push through them...persistence!

I think about that word now, and how he applied it to me, and now as a father, how I can apply that word and lessons to my children.

My son, Gabe, was born with some limitations. He couldn't walk, he couldn't crawl, and it scared the hell out of me and my beautiful wife, Danielle, to the point that when he was around a year old, we took him to Miami Children's Hospital and met with one of the country's top pediatric doctors to find out what the hell was going on.

It turns out Gabe was diagnosed with dyspraxia, which is a motor function disability. Although millions of people probably have it, dyspraxia isn't talked about much in this country. I'm convinced I had it as a kid. I had a difficult time doing the easiest things. For instance, I could never tie my shoes. But growing up in Brooklyn back when I did, they had no medical diagnosis for that. You were just considered spastic.

To put it in perspective: dyspraxia is to the United Kingdom what autism is to the United States. Here, everybody talks about autism and Autism Speaks, and very few people talk about dyspraxia. In England, it's the complete opposite. In fact, Daniel Radcliffe, the star of the *Harry Potter* movies, has dyspraxia.

So, at the Miami Children's Hospital, the doctor came up to me and said, "The good news is your son only has dyspraxia. The bad news is he's never going to lead the league in scoring, and he's never going to hit three hundred." I didn't find that funny. Not at all. My wife thought it was okay. I thought it was a real dick thing to say, you know? But at least now we knew what the problem was.

Thank God he doesn't suffer from a severe case of it and can still physically to do activities that doctors didn't think he'd be able to do as a child, like play basketball. Before COVID hit, we'd go to Riverside Park every day (the city closed the parks when COVID first appeared, which made no sense) and shoot jump shots and layups, and he'd smile at me, and I'd smile back. It was his way of telling me, "I got you, Dad. I got you." I think in that respect, me scoring a touchdown for my father and Gabe hitting a jump shot for me is the same thing, just a different generation.

Honestly, Danielle and I couldn't be prouder of him. I know every parent loves their kid and thinks their kid is the greatest, but Gabe is very special—as is my beautiful daughter, Ava, who is eighteen and on her way to college. Both my kids are walking definitions of "persistence." And I know my father is smiling down on them every day of their lives.

✪ ✪ ✪

I keep thinking about an old boxing analogy: It doesn't matter how many times you get knocked down on the canvas. What matters is what you do when you get back up. And I don't know if there's anyone in this business, I don't care if it's Howard Stern or Don Imus, that got knocked down nearly as often as I was, and not nearly in as embarrassing a fashion as I was, so if there was anybody in this business who has made a career out of getting knocked down (and sometimes from his own punch) and getting back up, it's yours truly. But the point is I still had to get back up, right? You gotta have persistence. If you stay on the canvas, it's over.

I gotta tell ya, there's a lot of guys in this business (and I'm not going to name names) who don't like me. (Hard to believe, right?) There are also a lot of guys in this business who are envious of me, and for some stupid reason, think they deserve my job. Thinking to themselves, That should be me! Sid isn't as good! He doesn't deserve these opportunities!

I mean, listen, guys work decades in this business to get a shot at WFAN. They'll work in Toledo, Ohio, in Clarksville, Tennessee. They'll do updates for thirty years to do a Saturday show on WFAN. Even my very talented friend Craig Carton bounced around a few cities before finding incredible success at WFAN with co-host Boomer Esiason, and now with Evan Roberts. I got there in two years. I was on Imus, I hosted a midday show, I did the Giants, and I didn't give a shit. It wasn't like I had to "make my bones" doing overnights in the third biggest market in Arkansas to get to WFAN.

I was good. I got there on raw talent. But, obviously, I never appreciated it, because I pissed it away. Everybody in the business thought the same thing, He had this great opportunity and just pissed it away because he couldn't control himself!

And now those same people are telling me, "Man, you've come back! This is a renaissance!" I mean, where I am now with the show I'm hosting on WABC, I'm literally talking to the most powerful people in the country on a daily basis, no bullshit. Interviewing top entertainers, actors, and athletes, as well as diving into movie and TV acting and writing this book.

The people who for years were putting me down are now calling me and singing a different tune, "Bro, I have to be honest. You've inspired me!" I think that's the persistence I'm talking about. That's the essence of what this book is.

Unlike my first book, which ended with me getting fired, living down in Boca Raton, Florida, and hoping, just hoping, to get back to WFAN in New York City. That was in 2010. And here we are twelve years later, and I mean, I don't want to quote James Cameron exactly, but why not? "I'm the king of the fucking world!"